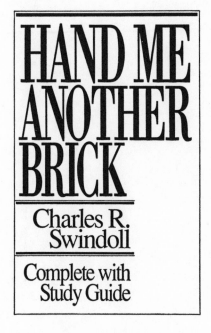

HAND ME ANOTHER BRICK

Charles R. Swindoll

Complete with Study Guide

OTHER NELSON BOOKS BY THE AUTHOR

Three Steps Forward, Two Steps Back–Expanded Edition
You and Your Child–Expanded Edition

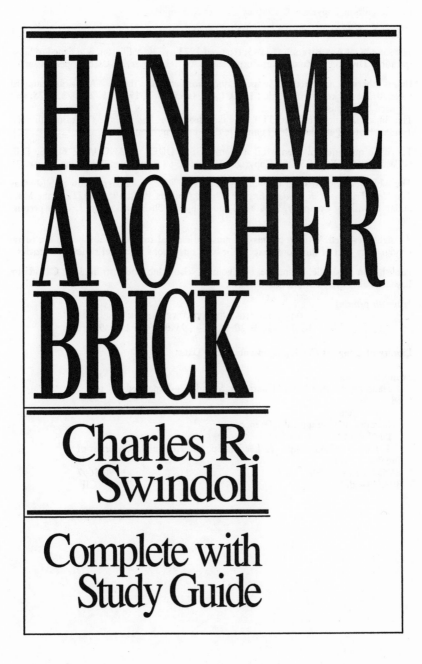

HAND ME ANOTHER BRICK

Charles R. Swindoll

Complete with Study Guide

Published in Nashville, Tennessee, by Thomas Nelson, Inc. and distributed in Canada by Lawson Falle, Ltd., Cambridge, Ontario.

Fifteenth printing
PRINTED IN THE UNITED STATES OF AMERICA.
15 16 17 18 19 20 21 — 95 94 93 92 91 90

Library of Congress Cataloging-in-Publication Data

Swindoll, Charles R.
    Hand me another brick / Charles R. Swindoll.—Expanded ed., rev. ed.
        p.   cm.
    Includes bibliographical references (p.
    ISBN 0-8407-3126-4 : $9.95
    1. Christian leadership. 2. Leadership. 3. Nehemiah (Governor of Judah) I. Title.
BV652.1.S94 1990   90-5657
303.3'4—dc20   CIP

This book is gratefully dedicated to the men on my staff whose loyalty I appreciate and whose leadership I admire. Each man models the message of this book.

Contents

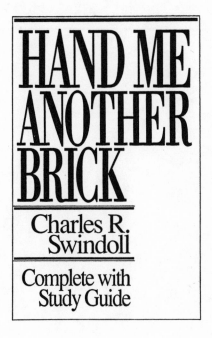

HAND ME ANOTHER BRICK

Charles R. Swindoll

Complete with Study Guide

Introduction

This is a practical book about leadership. My desire is threefold: (1) to be *accurate* with the facts as they relate to this subject and to Scripture, (2) to be *clear,* that is, non-technical and free from meaningless clichés, and (3) to be *relevant* and current in my comments, explaining how these ideas and suggestions can be implemented.

This is not a book of theory. I will leave the philosophical and psychological aspects of leadership and character development to the experts on the subject. My approach grows out of realistic observations I have made over the past twenty-five years in various areas of personal experience—a hitch in the U.S. Marine Corps (military leadership), several years in graduate school (educational leadership), employment in industry and business (labor and corporation leadership), almost two decades in churches, both in America and abroad (ecclesiastical leadership), and as a husband and father of four active children (domestic leadership).

As a student of the Bible, I continue to uncover more and more truth on this subject. It seems a shame to keep it hidden in my head or tucked away in my files, especially with so little being communicated about leadership from a *scriptural* perspective. Because I am convinced of the profound and powerful impact God's Word brings to those who glean its wisdom, I share these insights with genuine excitement.

My hope is to reach a broad cross-section of today's world—from the up-and-coming young person who is stimulated with the thought of leading others, to the top executive who lives in the threatening arena of difficult decisions and exhausting demands. It is out of a deep respect for these men and women, whose spheres of influence require long hours and disciplined thinking, that I write these words.

Being a leader is an unenviable calling. It appears glamorous and glorious—but it is more often lonely and thankless. As we shall see, the best leaders are actually servants. Unselfishly, they give of themselves to accomplish the objectives regardless of the sacrifice or cost. The perils are ever present and the toll is great. But so are the rewards, fleeting though they may be.

Originally, this material was presented to the attentive and responsive congregation of the church I serve as senior pastor, the First Evangelical Free Church in Fullerton, California. Shortly after I concluded the series in 1974, numerous friends and members asked me to put the material into print. Since that time I have shared the insights in a number of Bible conferences, on several Christian college campuses, and at seminars dealing with leadership. I cannot remember a time following such occasions when individuals did not urge me to make the series available in book form. At long last, I am pleased (and relieved!) to say it is done. It is doubtful I would have ever considered such an undertaking without the prodding of so many interested and encouraging people, Christians and non-Christians alike.

I appreciate, more than words can say, the editorial assistance of Brenda Arnold, whose counsel and suggestions proved invaluable. I am once again greatly indebted to Helen Peters for her secretarial assistance in transcribing the original material and then typing the final manuscript with such personal interest, remarkable speed, and devoted concern. And to my wife Cynthia, a constant partner, my source of stimulating encouragement and penetrating discussions, I freely declare my gratitude. Only she knows the relentless process of putting all these thoughts into words—and ultimately these words into a book.

To God be the glory.

C.R.S.

Fullerton, California
January, 1978

1
The Matter at Hand

Glance through today's newspaper and chances are good you will find another story of leadership breakdown. We no sooner had put Watergate to bed and finished wading through the Washington sex scandals than we were standing face to face with yet another delicate matter, called by some "Korea-gate"—foreign influence-peddling in the congressional arena.

The whole Ugandan crisis is basically a crisis of leadership. And the unveiling of a General Motors plant's substituting Chevrolet engines in certain models of Buicks and Oldsmobiles was, at the bottom line, a breakdown in leadership.

A similar scene exists today in many churches, Christian organizations, and educational institutions. Although things may appear smooth and stable on the surface, beneath the thin veneer it is not unusual to find internal strife or organizational confusion. Traditionalists versus innovators. Some yearn for new, fresh, less-structured approaches to meet the challenge of a more spontaneous generation of participants. Others prefer a fixed philosophy, staying with the status quo, steering clear of fads and ever-changing styles. The crying need for leadership comes through loud and clear.

So much of our personal frustration in daily living comes as a direct result of faulty leadership—tensions at work, communication breakdowns in the community, power struggles at the Tuesday night precinct meeting, and mismanagement of our children and homes.

What Is A Leader?

What do we mean when we use the word *leadership?* If I were asked to define it in one single word, the word would be *influence.* You lead someone to the measure you influence him.

The late President Harry Truman often referred to leaders as people who can get others to do what they don't want to do—and make them like doing it!

Reams of pages and stacks of books have been penned on the subject of leadership. There are few business and professional people who do not have a copy of Dale Carnegie's *How to Win Friends and Influence People,* a landmark volume on leadership and personal relationships. Another widely read book on this topic is Norman Vincent Peale's *Power of Positive Thinking.* Even books like *Winning Through Intimidation* and *I'm O.K., You're O.K.* relate to leadership in that they address the subject of handling person-to-person encounters.

A Manual For Leaders

However, there is one book, written about 425 B.C., that looms as a classic work on effective leadership; yet it is strangely obscure and virtually unknown to people of today. It was written by a man who was prominent in business and politics in the ancient Middle East. He not only possessed an exceptional personal philosophy of leadership, but he *lived it out* as well. In his lifetime, this gentleman rose from total obscurity to national recognition. His book bears his name: Nehemiah.

Believe it or not, what Nehemiah had to say concerning leadership speaks to the very same issues you and I face today. For example, from his book we learn—

- how to relate to a touchy boss
- the balance between faith in God and personal planning

- how to handle executive discouragement
- what to do with unwarranted criticism

In this biblical manual for potential leaders we find timeless and reliable guidelines that work. They enable us to know how to build quality characteristics in ourselves and others—the kind that are rarely seen today. These truths are not suddenly "dumped" on us, but rather they are modeled by Nehemiah as he accomplishes an incredible project against unbelievable odds.

As you get caught up in the story you will find yourself engaged in an imaginary dialogue, saying things like, "Nehemiah, you're my kind of guy. I need the characteristics that made you successful transferred into my own life. Hand me another brick, so I might reach my full potential and become all God planned for me to be!" Before coming to the end of the story, it will amaze you how many character bricks were passed from his hands to yours.

A Man To Match The Mountain

As far as leadership traits are concerned, Nehemiah was not that different from outstanding people whose names are far more familiar to us. Our nation's twenty-sixth president, for example, was a hard-charging leader. Throughout his days in office Theodore Roosevelt was either hated or admired. An ardent admirer once exclaimed to him, "Mr. Roosevelt, you are a great man!" In characteristic honesty he replied, "No, Teddy Roosevelt is simply a plain, ordinary man—highly motivated." It is safe to say that his answer describes most great leaders, including Nehemiah: plain and ordinary, yet *highly motivated.*

Edwin Markham expressed similar admiration for Abraham Lincoln: "Here was a man to hold against the world, a man to match the mountains and the sea."[1]

It doesn't sound as if such lofty words could describe an ordinary person, does it? But wait a minute. When God puts His hand on a plain, ordinary person whom He has destined for leadership, that person is given mountain-matching abilities, whether he be a

— 17 —

Roosevelt, a Lincoln, a Nehemiah—or a person like you or me. He motivates leaders to accomplish goals, to keep on working, to pass the bricks!

Nehemiah, although an ordinary man underneath, emerges as one of the most significant leaders in history. He was highly motivated to do a job for God that had many difficult circumstances surrounding it.

Before we get into the exciting specifics of learning effective leadership from Nehemiah, we need to get some quick history under our belts. Trying to study and appreciate Nehemiah without a knowledge of this transitional period of history would be like visiting old Concord Bridge in Massachusetts or the Liberty Bell in Philadelphia with no knowledge of the Revolutionary War. So take a moment in the remaining few pages of this chapter to catch a glimpse of what led up to the times in which Nehemiah lived. Then we will be ready for a careful study of Nehemiah the leader.

A Look At The Times

Jewish history begins with Abraham at approximately 2000 B.C. But it was not until one thousand years later that Israel took on world significance as a nation under Saul, David, and Solomon. In the successive reigns of these three kings, Israel's flag flew proudly over the nation. Israel was finally recognized as a major military power under King David's forty-year term of office.

David advanced the cause of Israel to remarkable proportions. Upon his death, David turned his throne over to his son Solomon. And if you know your Bible, you know that by the last part of his life Solomon had compromised so obviously with the world that God judged him.

So the Lord said to Solomon, "Because you have done this, and you have not kept My covenant and My statutes, which I have commanded you, I will surely tear the kingdom from you, and will give it to your servant. Nevertheless I will not do it in your days for the sake of your father David, but I will tear it out of the hand of your son" (1 Kings 11:11).

When Solomon died, there was a split in the nation's military ranks. Israel became a divided kingdom: ten tribes migrated to the north and settled in Samaria; the other two went south and settled in Jerusalem and the surrounding areas. The northern tribes during this period of division and civil war are called *Israel* and the southern group, *Judah*.

Just as the lowest ebb in American history was when we took up arms against each other in our Civil War, so it was with this north-south split in Jewish history. They reached their darkest hour nationally, not when they were attacked from without but when they were attacked from within, and the walls of their spiritual heritage began to crumble. During this time of division, literally all hell broke loose. Chaotic conditions prevailed.

God judged Israel when the Assyrians invaded in 722 B.C. Those ten tribes were finished; the Northern Kingdom ceased to exist. But some of the people from the north fled to the south to escape Assyrian control.

The land of Judah remained a Jewish nation for more than three hundred years. However, in 586 B.C. Babylon's King Nebuchadnezzar invaded Jerusalem (and all Judah) and took the people captive. This began what is called "The Babylonian Captivity." The biblical account in 2 Chronicles 36:18,19 records the end of Judah's history and the beginning of the Babylonian Captivity.

> And all the articles of the house of God, great and small, and the treasures of the house of the Lord, and the treasures of the king and of his officers, he [Nebuchadnezzar, the king of Babylon] brought them all to Babylon. Then they burned the house of God, and broke down the wall of Jerusalem and burned all its fortified buildings with fire, and destroyed all its valuable articles.

They burned the house of God, the temple, and they broke down the protective wall around the city. (Take special note of the words "house of God" and "the wall," for we want to deal with what they mean a bit later.) All the fortified buildings were destroyed with fire as were the valuable articles in the temple.

If you are a veteran of World War II, perhaps you saw Berlin or Tokyo at the end of the war. After the Babylonian takeover,

Jerusalem was in somewhat the same shape. It was totally leveled! The magnificent place where God's glory was once displayed was destroyed. The wall lay in ruins and wild dogs fed upon any edible remains. The armies of Babylon marched back home with all the treasures of Judah.

Psalm 137 was written during this dismal time. The psalmist cried out, "How can we sing the Lord's song in a foreign land?" (v. 4). Babylon had come and taken away the Israeli captives. Their song was ended. Second Chronicles 36:20 adds a final word:

> And those who had escaped from the sword he carried away to Babylon; and they were servants to him and to his sons until the rule of the kingdom of Persia.

That's important. Those Jews who lived through this siege of Jerusalem were bound together, chained like slaves, and sent to Babylon, a trek of more than eight hundred miles. And under Nebuchadnezzar and his wicked son, the Jews lived as they had centuries before in Egypt, as slaves to a foreign power.

But God didn't forget them. He had a purpose and a plan. Notice how verse 20 concludes: ". . . until the rule of the kingdom of Persia." Here's what happened There was a king named Cyrus who ruled Persia and another king, Darius, who ruled the neighboring Medes. The two nations were allies, but since the Persian force was the larger of the two, the two countries were often called simply "the kingdom of Persia." The Medes and the Persians invaded Babylon and overthrew it, forcing the Babylonian empire to surrender. What happened then? Second Chronicles 36:22 tells us; "Now in the first year of Cyrus king of Persia—in order to fulfill the word of the Lord by the mouth of Jeremiah—the Lord stirred up the spirit of Cyrus king of Persia." Was Cyrus a believer? No. On the surface he may have sounded like one, but he was not. He was, however, concerned for the welfare of the Jews. God is not limited to working with His people only. He works in the lives and minds of unbelievers whenever He chooses. He moves the hearts of kings from one plan to another. And this is what He did with Cyrus. God's ultimate plan was to get the Jews back into their land.

Cyrus sent a proclamation in writing throughout his kingdom, which said:

> Thus says Cyrus king of Persia, "The Lord, the God of heaven, has given me all the kingdoms of the earth, and He has appointed me to build Him a house in Jerusalem, which is in Judah. Whoever there is among you of all His people, may the Lord his God be with him, and let him go up!"

He was saying, "Let God's people go back—back to that city that was destroyed seventy years ago." This period of history has been called by some Bible historians "The Second Exodus." And so the Jews went back to Jerusalem under the leadership of three men.

"Company A" left first with Zerubbabel as their commanding officer. About eighty years later, another group, "Company B," left Babylon with Ezra as commander-in-chief. By now, Cyrus had died and Media-Persia was led by Artaxerxes. Then, thirteen years later, Nehemiah led "Company C" back to the destroyed city.

Remember I asked you to take special note of the terms "the house of God" and "the wall"? Here is the reason for that. I wanted you to remember "the house of God" because that is the main subject of the Book of Ezra and "the wall" of Jerusalem because that is the heart of the Book of Nehemiah. The Book of Ezra (which comes just before Nehemiah in the Old Testament) records how the house of God was rebuilt in the city of Jerusalem. But the temple was without protection for ninety years until God led Nehemiah to provide the leadership necessary to build a wall, and it is his account of that project that we call the Book of Nehemiah.

A Preview Of The Book

When we look at Nehemiah 1:3, we discover it holds great meaning: "The remnant there in the province who survived the captivity are in great distress and reproach, and the wall of Jerusalem is broken down and its gates are burned with fire." Nehemiah responded by saying, "Now it came about when I heard these words, I sat down and wept and mourned for days; and I was fasting and praying before the God of heaven" (v. 4).

In the Book of Nehemiah, the man who led his people is presented in three roles. Early in the book, he is the *cupbearer* to the king. Midway through the story, he is the *builder* of the wall. In the third part of the book, he is *governor* of the city and surrounding sections of Jerusalem.

The Cupbearer

King Artaxerxes is the man to whom Nehemiah reported as cupbearer. Being a cupbearer doesn't sound very impressive. The position sounds comparable to the dishwasher, or at best to the butler or the table waiter. But the cupbearer was far more important than that. The cupbearer tasted the wine before the king drank it, and he tasted the food before the king ate it. If the dinner was poisoned or if somebody was trying to slip the king a "mickey"—no more cupbearer, but long live the king. And through the practice of this custom, an incredible intimacy developed between the taster and the partaker, between the cupbearer and the king. In fact, it has been suggested by ancient historians that the cupbearer, like no one other than the king's wife, was in a position to influence the monarch.

One Old Testament scholar mentions that the cupbearer

> was often chosen for his personal beauty and attractions, and in ancient oriental courts was always a person of rank and importance. From the confidential nature of his duties and his frequent access to the royal presence, he possessed great influence.[2]

Many cupbearers used their office to make a few extra bucks by putting in a good word for guys in the field who wanted a governmental promotion or VIP treatment. The cupbearer was an intimate counsel to the king.

Nehemiah had established a good relationship with King Artaxerxes, but he had a burden on his heart. He needed a political favor himself! When he heard there was a wall broken down in Jerusalem, Nehemiah heard God saying to him, "I want you to be the leader in the building of that wall. You are My man for the job."

But rather than racing into the king's presence and saying, "God told me to go back to Jerusalem to build a wall. I'm God's man!" Nehemiah prayed for guidance. In fact, all through the book you will find Nehemiah asking the Lord for direction.

The Builder

Beginning in chapter 2, verse 11, we see Nehemiah change to his second hat; he became a *builder*, and a wise one at that.

New ideas seem to go through three channels. First, *rejection*. You have an idea for something new. The person you tell it to says, "It won't work." You ask, "Why?" He replies, "Because we've tried it before." Or, "No one's ever done that before." It's rejected. The second channel is *toleration:* "Well, I'll allow it, as long as . . . ." The third channel, the ideal response, is *acceptance:* "Let's go!"

Nehemiah, knowing the time was not right, didn't tell anybody that he was going to rebuild Jerusalem's wall. He got on his horse late at night (you can just see the moon shining on the ruins of the wall), and he said:

> I went out at night by the Valley Gate in the direction of the Dragon's Well and on to the Refuse Gate, inspecting the walls of Jerusalem which were broken down and its gates which were consumed by fire. Then I passed on to the Fountain Gate and the King's Pool, but there was no place for my mount to pass (Neh. 2:13,14).

Apparently the rubble was piled so high he couldn't get by on his horse. But he saw enough to know what had to be done—and to know how difficult the job would be. But he kept his plans to himself. "And the officials did not know where I had gone or what I had done; nor had I as yet told the Jews, the priests, the nobles, the officials, or the rest who did the work" (v. 16).

Chapters 3, 4, and 5 of the Book of Nehemiah tell us about the work of building the wall. In spite of great odds and internal and external enemies, they finished the job. The climax, the "ribbon-cutting," comes in Nehemiah 6:15: "So the wall was completed on the twenty-fifth of the month Elul, in fifty-two days."

The Governor

Finally, Nehemiah changed hats again. He became the *governor*. The account of his election is in chapter 5, but we don't read of delegation of authority until chapter 7, verse 1:

> Now it came about when the wall was rebuilt and I had set up the doors, and the gatekeepers and the singers and the Levites were appointed, that I put Hanani my brother, and Hanaiah the commander of the fortress, in charge of Jerusalem, for he was a faithful man and feared God more than many.

Nehemiah was a clear-thinking leader; he saw the importance of spiritual men at the helm of the city. Nehemiah also made a long list of the families in Jerusalem, starting with those who had returned first. They became the charter members of his new walled community.

Looking ahead to chapter 8, verse 9, we read:

> Then Nehemiah, who was the governor and Ezra the priest and scribe, and the Levites who taught the people said to all the people, "This day is holy to the Lord your God; do not mourn or weep." For all the people were weeping when they heard the words of the law.

Let's pause here and summarize. Nehemiah came into the city and rebuilt the wall. In chapter 8, we read that the people stood in a great court and asked that the book of the law of Moses be brought out. From a wooden pulpit Ezra read aloud to all the people. The people stood listening from early morning to midday and praised the name of their God.

You see, these people had been in captivity. They had been born to people in captivity. They had known spiritual desolation. And for the first time they saw their city showing signs of beginning anew. What an emotional moment it must have been when Ezra said, "Let's all stand and hear the Word of God." As he unrolled it and read from it, the people wept.

Nehemiah was the master bricklayer *and* general contractor! He changed from cupbearer to builder. When the wall was completed, despite the enemies, he established himself as governor and appointed godly men who would remind the people to purify themselves from sin and to praise God.

The Walls Of Our Lives

As we turn to look in detail at the characteristics of Nehemiah's leadership, consider a passage from Isaiah 49:15,16:

> Can a woman forget her nursing child,
> And have no compassion on the son of her womb?
> Even these may forget, but I will not forget you.
> Behold, I have inscribed you on the palms of My hands;
> Your walls are continually before Me.

God was saying to His people, "Your lives are like walls, continually before me. I have inscribed your life on my hands." What the walls were to Jerusalem, our lives are before God.

Quite frankly, I think the walls of our lives often lie in ruins through neglect. The leader who brings us to rebuild the walls is the Holy Spirit, and it is He who continues the work of reconstruction inside us. He tries His best to bring to our attention the condition of our walls, but sometimes we don't hear what He is saying. Yet, we are not hard of hearing; we simply don't listen.

Some of you are living within the walls of your life surrounded by ruin, and it all began very slowly. First there was a loose piece of stone or mortar. Then there was a crack that appeared in the wall. And then it broke into pieces, and there was a hole. Because of further neglect, the weeds of carnality began to grow through the wall. By and by, the enemy gained free access to your life.

You may be known as a good Christian. But you know in your heart that although you are a Christian in the same sense that Jerusalem belonged to the Jews, the wall around your spiritual life that protects and defends you is in shambles. Such things as selfishness, lack of discipline, procrastination, immorality, no time for God, compromise, and rebellion have come and sowed their ugly seeds. And they have begun to bear fruit for death.

Take serious inventory of your true condition. Before his project was ever undertaken, Nehemiah was informed and concerned. The first phase was *evaluation*. I sense in our day, among a number of people in the ranks of our evangelical family, a shallow frivolity concerning God. We tend to take Him lightly. It is as though He is our great big buddy. Then we hide behind the rationalization that "nobody is perfect." "After all," we tell ourselves, "I'm better than so-and-so and certainly better than I used to be." There's sort of a shrug of the shoulders and a passing comment, "Well, He'll understand." If this is your attitude, the enemy is living in your camp. Your walls are down.

Nehemiah's concern led him to the second phase, *reconstruction*. He prayed for guidance and correction. Have you been too busy for prayer?

"Oh, I've never been so busy! In all my life I've never been so busy."

But how about time with God?

You say, "Well, there's just not enough time in the day."

Get up earlier! Set aside the lunch hour. You cannot afford *not* to have time with God each day. It was said of Hudson Taylor that the sun never rose for forty years in China but that God didn't find him on his knees in prayer for that great land. Reconstruction, frankly, is hard work.

Consistency is the need of the hour. But erosion is our constant battle. Little by little, bit by bit, the process is set in motion. No one *suddenly* becomes base. Moral decay, as we have noted, takes place when the first piece of mortar comes loose and one stone drops to the side. You let it lie. Then another stone falls, and another.

Finally, Nehemiah honestly faced the situation and determined to stay with it until the task was done. The third phrase was *perseverance*. You may be ready to weep over your sin. You may be at the place of confessing your wrongdoing, even to someone else. But you have not come to the place where, as we read in Nehemiah, "the people had a mind to work." They determined to hang in there.

That leathery old saint, A. W. Tozer, put it so well:

Every farmer knows the hunger of the wilderness. That hunger which no modern farm machinery, no improved agricultural methods can quite destroy. No matter how well-prepared the soil, how well-kept the fences, how carefully painted the buildings, let the owner neglect for awhile his prized and valued acres and they will revert again to the wilds and be swallowed by the jungle or the wasteland. The bias of nature is toward the wilderness never toward the fruitful field.[3]

The neglected heart, the life with crumbled walls, will soon be overrun by the world and chaos will prevail. Don't just repent. *Rebuild!* Persevere! Never give up!

I'm deeply concerned that you do not read on, packing in theoretical facts on leadership, while you live without walls. If your heart has grown cold toward Christ and His church, deal with the problem now. Then as you read, expect the Holy Spirit to use the faith and persistence of Nehemiah to form within your heart a thirst and willingness to be the kind of leader that is blest by God.

2

A Leader—
From the Knees Up!

Like most people in leadership positions, Nehemiah continually faced impossible circumstances. You will remember that he was eight hundred miles from the concern on his heart: his people who lived in the midst of the destruction in Jerusalem. To live fifteen or twenty miles from where you work is one thing, but Nehemiah was faced with a sixteen-hundred-mile round trip! And who had ever heard of fifty-five miles per hour?

To further complicate matters, Nehemiah answered to an unbeliever—King Artaxerxes. Before Nehemiah could leave his responsible post and go to Jerusalem to build the wall, something had to be done in the heart of Artaxerxes. His mind needed changing. When Nehemiah received God's orders, he did not rush into the king's oval office and give him the mandate, "Three years' leave of absence or I quit!" Instead, he went before God in prayer and trusted him to open the doors and change the heart of his boss.

Here is how the story opens:

> The words of Nehemiah the son of Hacaliah. Now it happened in the month Chislev, in the twentieth year, while I was in Susa the capital, that Hanani, one of my brothers, and some men from Judah came; and I asked them concerning the Jews who had escaped and had survived the captivity, and about Jerusalem. And they said

to me, "The remnant there in the province who survived the captivity are in great distress and reproach, and the wall of Jerusalem is broken down and its gates are burned with fire." Now it came about when I heard these words, I sat down and wept and mourned for days; and I was fasting and praying before the God of heaven (Neh. 1:1–4).

Most likely, Nehemiah authored his book himself. He described himself simply as the son of Hacaliah, a man whose name does not appear elsewhere in Scripture. Nehemiah gave his occupation in verse 11 of the opening chapter: "I was the cupbearer to the king." That is all we know about his earthly credentials. He was the cupbearer to the king, and he was the son of Hacaliah.

A Cupbearer with a Heart for God

As we noted in the previous chapter, being a cupbearer meant he was the wine and food taster. He served as the screen between the public and the king. It was a position of intimacy and trust.

The story opens in the winter time; it was the month of Chislev, or December, in the twentieth year of the king. Looking back, we know the year was about 445–444 B.C. And the place is given to us in verse 1: Nehemiah lived in Susa, the capital of the Media-Persian empire, the Washington, D.C. of the day. Even more significantly, Susa was recognized by the Jews as the capital of the then-known world. It was a hub of activity, the place of ultimate decision-making; often late-breaking news of the empire came to King Artaxerxes' attention through the lips of his cupbearer. Nehemiah was the king's right-hand man.

In verse 2, Hanani, one of Nehemiah's brothers (I take this to mean one of his blood brothers), and some men from Judah came. "And I [Nehemiah] asked them concerning [please notice the two questions:] [1] the Jews who had escaped and had survived the captivity, and [2] about Jerusalem."

It has been said that the true Jew never completely forgets Jerusalem. This was certainly true of Nehemiah. He wanted to know about the people; he wanted to know the condition of the beloved city. Those returning from Judah told him: "The remnant [the people] there in the province who survived the captivity are in great distress and reproach." The Hebrew word translated *great distress* means "misery" and "calamity." The people who were in that city were in a vulnerable position. In fact, the men added, they were under *reproach*. The Hebrew word means "sharp," "cutting," "penetrating," or "piercing." The idea is one of bearing the brunt of cutting words. The Jews were being criticized and slandered by people who were enemies of the faith.

Nehemiah was brokenhearted. Verses 4 through 11 contain his reaction, and it is here we begin to see his gift of leadership unfold. I am deeply impressed with the fact that though he was in a high-ranking position in the world, he had a heart that was very tender toward God. You know, it's a tough combination to find a person who holds a high position in the eyes of the world and yet who is tender before God.

Perhaps you are in a position of great importance. It's a vulnerable place to live. Each promotion further endangers your spiritual life, your position threatens your walk with God. It doesn't *have* to cripple your walk, but it can be, and often is, damaging. All through Scripture, there are accounts of people who were promoted from one level to the next and suffered from "promotion erosion"—they slowly became lost in pride. I deal with this problem at length in chapter 8.

Marks of a Competent Leader

Nehemiah, touched by the need of his people, "sat down and wept and mourned . . . and I was fasting and praying before the God of heaven" (v. 4). In verses 4 through 11, there are four very significant factors revealed that are true in the lives of competent, spiritual leaders. I want you to remember them, so I will list them as they occurred in Nehemiah's experience. Let's take them in order.

1. A Leader Has a Clear Recognition of the Needs.

The beginning of verse 4 reads, "It came about when I heard these words." Nehemiah was not preoccupied; he did not live in a dreamworld, opposed to reality. He asked, "What's the condition?" They replied, "It's a miserable situation." He heard what they said.

You may think recognizing needs is an elementary concept, especially for leaders. But I have met many people in responsible leadership positions who never seem to see the problems they ought to be solving.

I remember taking a course in seminary under a brilliant Bible teacher. In fact, he was known all over the world for his knowledge of Scripture. But he was so well-read and had known the answers for so long that he had forgotten there could be any questions! We would raise our hands and pose a problem, and he would blink and say, "Problem? What problem?"

There is a very simple reason for this "no problem" mentality: preoccupation. Have you ever been around a preoccupied professor or boss? Some of you live with preoccupied husbands, and you know getting his attention is no easy task. You look at him behind the *Wall Street Journal* and say, "Honey, I want to talk with you about something that's happened."

"Uh huh."

"It's leaking . . . in the other room . . . it's running out onto the floor."

"Uh huh."

It's remarkable how individuals who have a high level of responsibility often can no longer relate at the problem level.

I have a friend who is quite successful in the construction business. In fact, he is a prominent builder in his city. But he *hates* reality. As a result, his family has suffered. He has been deceived and ripped off and misused time and again because he hates to face issues and refrains from asking the hard, second questions. He is creative, visionary, warm, loving, very tender personally toward the things of God. But he just doesn't see *the problems*. He avoids confrontation with them by saying, "Don't tell me the problems; let's talk about the good things."

Now I think a person can be so problem-oriented that problems are all he can think about—and that's not good either. But the person who is a real leader has a clear recognition of the needs.

Are you aware of needs? How about the needs in your own

family? Are you sensitive as a parent or as a mate? Maybe you live alone. Do you know what is on your parents' hearts, where the scales tip? If you teach, are you aware of the pupils' needs—the kids who fill your classroom? If you are in business leadership, are you in touch with more than just that level of pleasurable activity called the "executive stratum"? What about those other areas where problems start and fester?

2. A Leader Is Personally Concerned with the Need.

Nehemiah went a step beyond recognition of the problem. He not only heard these matters, but he also sat down and identified with them.

Alan Redpath once wrote:

> Let us learn this lesson from Nehemiah: you never lighten the load unless first you have felt the pressure in your own soul. You are never used of God to bring blessing until God has opened your eyes and made you see things as they are.[4]

There is no better preparation for Christian service than that.

Nehemiah was called to build the wall, but *first he wept over the ruins.* "The walls are down. Oh, God! How can these walls be down and these people continue in safety?" But the *normal* response is, "Oh, the walls are down! Who fouled up? Who blew it?" Or, "They've been back there all these years and nobody has built those walls? Send me their names; I'll deal with them." These reactions are wrong. A leader must have compassion.

Before I go any further, I want us to learn a very practical lesson about a father who refused to recognize a specific family need. The story is found in 1 Samuel 3. All through my childhood, I remember being told in Sunday school about young Samuel who was asleep on his cot when somebody said, "Samuel! Samuel!" And he ran over to Eli and said, "What is it?" And Eli said, "Go back to sleep. It was not I." Again, the voice woke Samuel, and the same thing happened. Finally, Eli said, "Listen, that's God you're hearing." And the story always ended there.

I wondered, "Why in the world did God wake him so often?

What was the Lord trying to tell him?" Later I found the answer in verses 11 and 12:

> And the Lord said to Samuel, "Behold, I am about to do a thing in Israel at which both ears of everyone who hears it will tingle. In that day I will carry out against Eli all that I have spoken concerning his house, from beginning to end."

Don't tell me God isn't concerned about a leader's home. Here was Eli, a spiritual leader in Israel, and God's concern was over his home. Read verse 13:

> For I have told him that I am about to judge his house forever [notice] for the iniquity which he knew, because his sons brought a curse on themselves and he did not rebuke them.

Underline in your Bible "he knew" and "he did not rebuke them." Are there times when you know something wrong is going on at your house, but you refuse to be involved in correcting it? We carelessly pull the shades on reason and say, "Well, somehow it's going to work out."

Listen, God has appointed the father to one of the most difficult leadership positions in all the world: to lead his home. He motivates, sets the pace, gives guidance and encouragement, and handles discipline. Eli knew all this, but he would not rebuke his sons when they disobeyed God. Maybe he figured the leaders at the temple would straighten out the kids. It's tragic how many people leave the job of child-rearing to the church, and therefore the church lives under the constant indictment, "The worst kids in the world are the church kids." The church gets the blame. But it's not a church problem; it's a *home* problem. The church can seldom resurrect what the home puts to death.

As we turn back to Nehemiah as a model for leadership, realize that we are not talking only about Nehemiah and some ancient city at the dawn of history. We are talking about *today*. The higher you get in the echelon of what the world calls success, the easier it is to fade into theoretical preoccupation and to leave the realistic "lesser things" to themselves.

Notice, in verse 4, that Nehemiah was "fasting and praying." What does it mean to fast? It means to miss a meal for one major purpose: zeroing in on your walk with God. Some people fast one day a week. Some people fast a day a month. Some never fast. Interestingly, it is mentioned rather frequently in Scripture. When our motive is right, it is amazing what we can accomplish with the Lord when we occasionally save the time of fixing, eating, and cleaning up after a meal and invest it on our knees. The more responsibility we shoulder, the more time we need for contemplation before our Father.

3. A Serious Leader Goes First to God with the Problem.

In verse 5 we hear Nehemiah say, "I beseech Thee, O Lord God of heaven." He prayed.

What is your first response when a need comes to your attention? I can tell you what it is because it's usually my first response in my own fallen human nature: "How can I work this out?" or "What did so-and-so do wrong to make that happen?"

Your people problem, whatever it may be, will not be completely solved until you take it to God in prayer. I mentioned this in the first chapter, and it is illustrated in Nehemiah's life. Someday you will look back at those things you did rationally in the flesh, and you will hate the day you did them. Prayer, I repeat, is absolutely essential in the life of a leader.

Look at how Nehemiah behaved before the Lord. First, he *praised God.*

> I beseech Thee, O Lord God of heaven, the great and awesome God, who preserves the covenant and lovingkindness for those who love Him and keep His commandments (verse 5).

He knew he was not coming to just another man, but rather to the God of heaven.

For whom did Nehemiah work? The king. Was this king great and mighty on the earth? The mightiest! But compared to God, King Artaxerxes was nothing. And so it stands to reason that when we go to God in prayer, we put things into proper perspective. If you are having difficulty loving or relating to an individual, take him to God. Bother the Lord with this person. Don't you be bothered with him—leave him at the throne.

Next, in verses 6 and 7, he *confessed his part in the problem.*

> Let Thine ear now be attentive and Thine eyes open to hear the prayer of Thy servant which I am praying before Thee now, day and night [not just a quick panic prayer, but day and night], on behalf of the sons of Israel Thy servants, confessing the sins of the sons of Israel which we have sinned against Thee; I and my father's house have sinned. We have acted very corruptly against Thee.

Notice the words "we" and "I." The confession was not on behalf of someone else's failure. The confession had to do with Nehemiah's part in the problem. What do we do when we are in conflict with another person? We usually blame the other person (our fallen state coming through again). We usually think of six or seven ways the other person has manifested his stubbornness and unwillingness to change, but we seldom consider our part in the problem. But it works both ways. So the very first thing Nehemiah said in regard to the problem was, "Lord, I am culpable. I am not only wanting to be part of the answer, I am confessing myself to be part of the problem."

There may be husband-wife difficulties at your house or strained pupil-teacher relationships at school. There might be strife between a parent and child. And invariably, you will think of your mate or your child or your mom or your teacher or your pupil as being the problem. That is not necessarily the truth.

I plead with you—as you go before God in prayer concerning any unresolved personality conflicts, have the attitude reflected in these words: "Lord, I bring before you these areas where *I* have caused an irritation. This is *my* realm of responsibility. I can't change him. But God, I can tell you that this is my part in it; forgive me."

Nehemiah didn't stop with confession. Next, he *claimed the promise.* When he went to God in prayer, he praised the Father, confessed his part in the wrong, and claimed the promise God had given.

Verse 8 reads "Remember the word which Thou didst command Thy servant Moses." What was Nehemiah doing? He was quoting a verse of Scripture to God. He quoted not only from Leviticus 26 but also from Deuteronomy 30. He knew the Book. "Lord, I open the Book before You. I bring You the very words You spoke, the promise You made. And I'm claiming it, Lord, right now."

What was the promise? It was twofold. The promise was that if Israel disobeyed, they would go into a foreign land. That had come to pass. The second part was that when that time of captivity was ended God would bring the Jews back to Jerusalem and protect them. That part was unfulfilled. So Nehemiah was saying, "Lord, the first part is true. We've disobeyed and we've been in captivity. But, Lord, You made a promise to bring us back into the city and protect us, and that has not come to pass yet. I am claiming that it will."

The apostle Paul wrote:

> Yet, with respect to the promise of God, he [Abraham] did not waver in unbelief, but grew strong in faith, giving glory to God, and being fully assured that what He had promised, He was able also to perform (Rom. 4:20,21).

God does not lightly give out promises. He says, "I promise you that if you will give Me your burden, I will bear it. If you will seek first My kingdom, I will add all these other things to you. If you will make your heart right before Me, I will lead you into a path of stability and prosperity."

That doesn't necessarily mean He will fill your wallet. It does mean He will give you peace—like the world is not able to know. "I will promote you to a place of My level of significance, and you will be satisfied."

Nehemiah said, "Lord, You promised that Your people will be protected in that city, and I'm claiming it right now."

Finally Nehemiah *brought his petition or desire before God*. His petition was a bold one.

> O Lord, I beseech Thee, may Thine ear be attentive to the prayer of Thy servant and the prayer of Thy servants who delight to revere

Thy name, and make Thy servant successful today, and grant him compassion before this man (v. 11).

Have you ever prayed this? "Lord, make me successful. Make me find that place in the center of Your will where heavenly prosperity rests, in whatever level it may be. May I reach the maximum so that I am, in Your eyes, prosperous. And, Lord, grant me favor with those in authority over me!" That's bold petitioning.

4. A Leader Is Available to Meet the Need Himself.

"Make me successful. Grant *me* compassion in his eyes." Nehemiah *recognized* the need clearly. He got *involved* in it. He *took it to God*. Now he was *available* to meet the need, if that was what God desired.

A genuine leader is marked by diligent faithfulness in the midst of a task. And that faithfulness is more than passive inclination. It is demonstrated by being available and personally involved in meeting needs. There is not much benefit in leadership by proxy.

During my days in the Marine Corps we were often told that a captain stays with his company and a squad leader stays with his squad. As the intensity of the battle increases, the more his presence means. Those in command were instructed to be available, to get involved. Continued aloofness among military leaders weakens the morale of those under their command.

Leaders in God's work would do well to remember that principle. Prayer is primary. But not theoretical prayer. Prayer that gets the job done includes the conviction, "I'm available, Lord—ready and willing."

Benefits of Prayer

Nehemiah 1 is a blend of prayer and action. All who lead must place a high priority on prayer. Why is prayer so important? Here are the four shortest reasons I know.

Prayer *makes me wait*. I cannot pray and work at the same time. I have to wait to act until I finish praying. Prayer forces me to leave the situation with God; it makes me wait.

Secondly, prayer *clears my vision*. Southern California often has an overhanging weather problem in the mornings because of its coastal location until the sun "burns through" the morning fog. Prayer does that. When you first face a situation, is it foggy? Prayer will "burn through." Your vision will clear so you can see through God's eyes.

Thirdly, prayer *quiets my heart*. I cannot worry and pray at the same time. I am doing one or the other. Prayer makes me quiet. It replaces anxiety with a calm spirit. Knees don't knock when we kneel with them!

Fourthly, prayer *activates my faith*. After praying I am more prone to trust God. And how petty and negative and critical I am when I don't pray! Prayer sets faith on fire.

Don't just fill the margins in your Bible with words and thoughts about ways a leader prays. Do it! Don't stop with just a sterile theology of prayer. Pray! Prayer was the first major step Nehemiah took in his journey to effective leadership.

> Got any rivers you think are uncrossable?
> Got any mountains you can't tunnel through?
> God specializes in things thought impossible,
> He does the things others cannot do.[5]

The Lord is the Specialist we need for these uncrossable and impossible experiences. He delights in accomplishing what we cannot pull off. But He awaits our cry. He listens for our request. Nehemiah was quick to call for help. His favorite position when faced with problems was the kneeling position.

How about you?

3

Preparation for a Tough Job

There are few areas of life in which we live or work that do not come ready-equipped with a superior—a boss or other authority figure. Student, teacher, nurse, executive, salesman, airline pilot, coach, chef, or scientist all have immediate superiors whose presence significantly controls and affects their lives. It is our task to develop qualities of leadership germinating within ourselves while still being accountable to these superiors in our individual spheres of influence. That isn't easy! Leaders are usually better at leading than being led.

The question remains: *When that time of confrontation comes*—between boss and employee, parent and child, coach and player, teacher and pupil—*how do we handle it?* That question becomes increasingly complex when the superior is insensitive to or unconcerned with spiritual things.

Hudson Taylor once said, "It is possible to move men through God by prayer alone." As a leader, you will come to places where those in authority over you are beyond your power to change. The message God has for you at that point is prayer.

Proverbs 21 is an interesting proverb for a couple of reasons. First, it is a comparative proverb in which something is likened to something else. Most comparative proverbs end with the comparison and leave it at that. But this proverb comes to a conclusion in what could be called the declarative part of the proverb. It concludes with a timeless principle, but let's first consider the comparison.

A Proverb With Punch

"The king's heart is like channels of water in the hand of the Lord." The Hebrew sentence does not begin with "The king's heart . . ." but with the word "channels," referring to small irrigation ditches that run from a main reservoir to dry, thirsty flatlands that need to be filled with water. "Like irrigation canals carrying water is the heart of the king in Jehovah's hand," the original says. But what does this proverb tell us about our superiors? The writer was saying that the heart that breathes out and communicates decisions and attitudes is in the Lord's hand. That is, God is sovereign.

Now look at the last part of the proverb, the declaration: "He [Jehovah] turns it wherever He wishes."

The Lord has in His hand the heart of a king. (Whether the king is a believer or not is unimportant.) Because the Lord has the king's heart in His hand, He literally "causes it to be bent" wherever He is pleased. So putting it all together, the verse could read, "Like irrigation canals carrying water, so is the heart of the king in Jehovah's hand. He causes it to bend and incline in whatever direction He pleases."

What is true of the king is true of your superior! To understand your boss, you must become acquainted with God's method of operation; for the Lord has the heart of your superior in His hand. Pause momentarily and rivet that thought in your mind.

A Boss Who Won't Budge

We will see how the story of Nehemiah beautifully illustrates the truth revealed in Proverbs 21:1. Nehemiah worked under a man who just happened to be the king of Persia. There's a saying that goes, "Don't try to change it. It's like the law of the Medes and the Persians," and it means that something is impossible to change! Artaxerxes, king of the Medes and the Persians, had a reputation for being impossible to change. Nehemiah was in an influential position, for he played an intimate part in the king's life. But Nehemiah's heart was not in Persia; it was in Jerusalem. He wanted to go back to his beloved city and rebuild those walls, but he couldn't just leave his job. God had to work through the heart of the king if Nehemiah was to expect Artaxerxes to be receptive to his personal request.

Nehemiah sought the Lord in prayer because he knew that was the only way to change the king's heart. He prayed intently, "O Lord, I beseech Thee, may Thine ear be attentive to the prayer of Thy servant and the prayer of Thy servants who delight to revere Thy name" (Neh. 1:11). Now look at his request: "And make Thy servant successful today, and grant him compassion before this man." Nehemiah, cupbearer to the king, said in effect, "Lord, I ask You to change the heart of the king; alter his attitudes. Change the situation so that I may be allowed to do Your will with his pleasure—the pleasure of my superior." He didn't rashly run to Jerusalem, but he laid his problem before God.

Waiting is Essential

What happened after Nehemiah prayed to the Lord? Nothing! At least not right away. Nehemiah's story opened in the month of Chislev (see Neh. 1:1), and it resumes "in the month of Nisan" (Neh. 2:1). Chislev is December; Nisan is April. For four months nothing happened.

Have you ever had that disillusioning experience? Perhaps you heard the preacher say one Sunday, "Just pray to God; give Him the situation." So you went home and prayed about a frustrating problem and ended with the favorite American prayer: "Lord, give me patience—and I want it NOW!" Then Monday morning came and nothing changed; what's worse, a *month* from then, nothing had changed. "Lord, are You awake? Did You hear me?" you ask. Another month passes, and then another. That was Nehemiah's experience.

The prayer warrior quickly learns the patience of waiting. And so Nehemiah was doing just that—waiting. In the diary he kept, nothing was entered for those four months because nothing happened. He waited. There was no visible glimmer of hope, no change. He kept waiting and trusting and counting on God to move the heart of his superior.

Now look at verse 1 of chapter 2: "And it came about in the month Nisan, in the twentieth year of King Artaxerxes, that wine was before him, and I took up the wine and gave it to the king." The Living Bible emphasizes the waiting period: "One day in April four months later."

Here Nehemiah was in a familiar situation. The king and his queen were reclining together, having finished their sumptuous meal. The delightful aroma of the food permeated the room. Nehemiah poured them some of their favorite vintage from the vine and brought it to them. "I took up the wine and gave it to the king," Nehemiah said, adding an insightful statement: "Now I had not been sad in his presence."

Do you know how to tell when someone wants you to know he has been spending long hours in prayer? Look at him. If he wants to show you how very spiritual he is, he wears his "super-pious look," usually evidenced by a *long* face.

But Nehemiah didn't have that gloomy glare. For four months he did not show that face. Incredible, isn't it? If we were to spend three or four hours on our knees, we would get up with a face that tells everyone we've been praying earnestly about something. Nehemiah had left his concern with the Lord, saying, "Lord, take over. It's Your timing; I'm going to rest it with You." Consequently, he could honestly report, "I had not been sad in his [the king's] presence."

Four months, however, can seem a long time to wait for some sign of response from the Lord. Everybody's got a breaking point. Nehemiah had come to the place where he had just begun to wonder, "Is it ever going to happen?" Maybe this was his blue Monday, for Nehemiah was rather sad when he served the royal couple that day. And the king said to him: "Why is your face sad though you are not sick? This is nothing but sadness of heart! Then I [Nehemiah] was very much afraid" (v. 2).

I appreciate Nehemiah's honesty. Many leaders no longer admit their human weaknesses. Not Nehemiah. He honestly said, "When the king said that to me, I got scared." No matter how great you may become, it is important you let the cracks in your life show. Rather than hiding them—admit them!

Nehemiah had good reason to be frightened. Subjects who were noticeably sad or melancholic in the presence of the king were usually killed for "raining on his parade." Keep Nehemiah's feelings in mind as you read verses 3 and 4:

> And I said to the king, "Let the king live forever. Why should my face not be sad when the city, the place of my fathers' tombs, lies desolate and its gates have been consumed by fire?"
> Then the king said to me, "What would you request?" [That's the moment Nehemiah has been awaiting! God opened the door.] So I prayed to the God of heaven.

And Nehemiah instantly prayed, asking the Lord for wisdom in choosing words to express his desire to the king.

Have you ever been in the midst of answered prayer? You prayed and waited, prayed and waited, and finally the door swung open. For a brief moment you stood there almost unable to believe the reality of the answer. Your mind raced as you spontaneously sought God's leading: "O God, this is such a critical point. Help me to take these steps very carefully."

That's precisely where Nehemiah was at this juncture in the story. God had thrown the door wide open.

"What would you request?" Artaxerxes asked Nehemiah. The king's heart was in the hands of Jehovah. God had adjusted the thinking of King Artaxerxes so that he was receptive to his employee's wishes. "What do you want, Nehemiah? What's worth getting sad over?"

Nehemiah responded (v. 5): "If it please the king, and if your servant has found favor before you, send me to Judah, to the city of my fathers' tombs, that I may rebuild it." That's Nehemiah's answer, his request. He had sought the Lord's help to "change the heart of the king." He had patiently waited four long months for His answer. And now his petition was granted. He made known his desire.

Nehemiah bared his heart before his boss and waited for his

response. It was not long in coming. Nehemiah wrote, "The king said to me, the queen sitting beside him."

Now, why in the world, we ask ourselves, did Nehemiah take the trouble to point out the queen's presence? It really makes one wonder, doesn't it? In Hebrew, the word translated *queen* here actually means "a close intimate friend," "a contact," or "a consort." Maybe the queen leaned over to her husband and whispered something. Maybe he first spoke with her, and she gave the king the nudge he needed. Whatever happened, the king's response was, "How long will your journey be, and when will you return?" The last of verse 6 reads: "I gave him a definite time."

This tells me the king didn't want Nehemiah to stay away. He was doing a good job as cupbearer. Despite his concern for Jerusalem, Nehemiah's attitude at work was positive. He was a diligent worker. That, my friend, is a rare person! When your heart is somewhere else, it is really difficult to perform the task at hand. But for four months, Nehemiah had faithfully done his job, and so the king didn't think, "Man, I've been looking for a way to get rid of him. Now's my chance. Go on to Jerusalem." Instead, he asked, "When will you come back?"

Look at Nehemiah's marvelous response: "I gave him a definite time." That's great! I weary of people who call it "faith" when they can't tell you their plans. Have you ever heard an individual say, "No, we're not going to think this through. We're just going by 'faith.' God will lead us." The calculating businessman says, "Uh huh, yeah. You'll be back needing more bucks before you're halfway there." The presence of faith does not mean an absence of organization.

God Honors A Plan

"I gave him a definite time."

Do you know that God honors order and organization? Can you imagine what had previously transpired in Nehemiah's mind in order for him to provide an immediate, on-the-spot answer? Nehemiah had a plan. You see, he had been doing more than praying for four months. He had been planning. That in itself was an exercise in faith. He was so sure God would let him go that he even drew up an agenda in case the king asked him how much leave of absence he would need!

Proverbs 16:9 says,

> The mind of man plans his way,
> But the Lord directs his steps.

Going out by faith doesn't mean you're going out in a disorderly or haphazard manner. You think through a project and count the cost financially. (I deal with this issue at length in Chapter 7.)

It is of great concern to me that so many people who undertake some project in the Lord's work enter without careful planning. They abruptly begin without thinking through questions such as: "Where will this lead us? How can I express this in clear, unmistakable, concrete terms? What are the costs, the objectives, the possible pitfalls? What process should be used?" I could name a number of individuals or families who entered the ministry with enthusiasm but later dropped out because they had not considered the cost. The most disillusioned people I know are those in the Lord's work who are paying the price of not thinking through their plans.

Admittedly, planning is hard work. Thinking isn't as exciting as involvement, but without it confusion is inevitable. Good leaders do their homework!

Some may read Nehemiah 2:7–9 and think Nehemiah presumptuous. No, he's practical. When King Artaxerxes said, "Fine. You may go," Nehemiah continued, "Now wait a minute, King, before I leave there are a couple of things I want to talk about."

> If it please the king [I like the gracious way he starts], let letters be given me for the governors of the provinces beyond the River [the governors were people who were going to attempt to stop him in his plan], . . . and a letter to Asaph the keeper of the king's forest, that he may give me timber to make beams for the gates of the fortress which is by the temple, for the wall of the city, and for the house to which I will go.

What's he asking for? He's asking for timber to build himself a house. That's a practical mind at work. You see, during these four months of waiting, Nehemiah was planning.

The old Revolutionary War soldiers used to say, "Trust in God, but keep your powder dry." Pray to God, but make your plans, set your sights, think through the hurdles.

Many people in God's work are shortsighted. Imagine Nehemiah's conversation with the first official outside the province of Susa if he had not planned ahead.

"Where are you going?"

"Well, I was hoping by faith to go to Jerusalem."

"Okay, where are your letters?"

"I don't have any letters."

"Then go back and get them."

So, he would have had to go back and start all over.

Nehemiah was unlike the majority of "faith workers." Can't you picture him as he rode out of Susa and approached the first official?

"Here's a letter from the king."

"Who wrote it?"

"Artaxerxes. See . . . right there."

"Oh, man! Go on through."

Next, he entered Asaph's territory. Asaph was probably a negative thinker and maybe a tightwad.

"What do you want?"

"I want some timber."

"Nope! Only by requisition."

"Artaxerxes requisitioned me to have all the timber I want."

I'm sure Asaph checked out that requisition!

That's an example of perfect planning. God honors that kind of thinking.

King Artaxerxes' positive response is stated in verse 6: "So it pleased the king to send me." Artaxerxes had to send him, for God was on Nehemiah's side. It was just a matter of time. So Artaxerxes said, "That's fine. You may go." But did he stop there? Verse 8 concludes with the sentence, "And the king granted them to me. . . ." He granted the letters—official "tickets" to get him through.

Notice Nehemiah's insight in his reason for the king's response: "And the king granted them to me because the good hand of my God was on me." For four months, in the solitude of his prayer closet, Nehemiah had faithfully bombarded the throne of God: "Lord, send me to Jerusalem. Change the heart of the king so that I can go. Give me the green light!" And so Nehemiah had no doubt about the reason for this turn in events.

When the Lord has His hand on His appointed leaders, it's like a sweeping wind as people are moved to respond. The Lord's hand was upon Nehemiah—and off he went, excited as he could be.

A Long Journey

Look at him enroute. Verse 9 begins: "Then I came to the governors of the provinces beyond the River." There they are, just as he had expected. Nehemiah gave them the *king's* letters. Not only did the king send letters, but he also provided for Nehemiah over and above anything he had requested: "Now the king sent with me officers of the army and horsemen."

The king offered to do more than Nehemiah had ever expected. "I'll not only send letters. I'll not only send you the okay to use my timber. I'll dispatch a few horsemen and a few soldiers, and they can go right along with you to protect you on your way."

The king's gracious response came because his heart was in Jehovah's hand. God bent it wherever He pleased.

Nehemiah was on the way toward his goal, but in verse 10 we learn he came face to face with tough characters, the same ones he will run across again and again throughout the project. Look at them.

> And when Sanballat the Horonite and Tobiah the Ammonite official heard about it, it was very displeasing to them that someone had come to seek the welfare of the sons of Israel (v. 10).

Nehemiah faced his first opposition. When you walk by faith, you will invariably collide with the "Sanballats" and the "Tobiahs."

If you have attempted any project requiring volunteer labor, you have encountered people who never tire of quoting Murphy's Law: "It won't work." Many men and women live by that principle. Their whole life is one big negative. They have a critical spirit that smothers them. Whenever a challenge comes their way, they respond, "It can't be done!"

So when Sanballat and Tobiah heard about Nehemiah's coming, their immediate response was "No way!" You see, in addition to their negative attitudes, they had business investments with the citizens of Jerusalem, and Nehemiah's plan was sure to hurt their pocketbooks. And they began to make plans to oppose God's arrangement.

When you walk by faith and seek to lead, you will encounter the hostility of people who walk by sight. They are rebuked by the life of faith. They are especially rebuked because they don't have your vision. Sanballat and Tobiah heard about Nehemiah's ambitious plans to rebuild the city walls, and they were disturbed. Experiencing criticism and opposition doesn't necessarily mean you are outside God's will. Rather, it may reinforce the fact that you are in the very center of His plan.

As we saw in chapter 1, it was here Nehemiah "changed hats." No longer the cupbearer, he was now the construction engineer—the chief bricklayer. "So I came to Jerusalem and was there three days" (2:11).

What was Nehemiah doing? We don't know. But judging from Nehemiah's track record, he was probably back before God seeking further direction.

Four Principles on Preparation

Nehemiah was preparing for a tough job, but he had his head on straight. The account of his preparation reveals what I consider to be four timeless principles for getting started God's way.

1. Changing a Heart Is God's Speciality.

Do not—I repeat—*do not* try to change people to fit your specifications. Don't try to manipulate people, play games, plan schemes, trick, or deceive them. Instead, tell God on them! You may have a spouse who is just plain ornery, and you were told this very morning that he or she does not plan to change! Let God deal with your mate's stubbornness.

Perhaps you are working with someone who is unfair and unbending, just plain *unreal*. How are you going to work in this situation? You've tried every manipulative move in the world without success. Talk to God about him or her.

You may know people in business or at school who are impossible creatures! God says, "Let Me at them. I will change them in ways you never would believe possible. Now, I'm not going to do it according to *your* timetable. I'm going to do it in My time." So between now and then, just relax.

But in the meantime, don't look so spiritual! When your spouse looks at you and says, "What are you doing?" don't turn to him or her with your eyelids at half-mast and say with a syrupy-sweet tone, "I'm just praying for you, Honey, that God will change your life."

That's *terrible* stuff! Just relax; let God take care of it. Then when change comes, guess who gets *all* the glory.

2. Praying and Waiting Go Hand in Hand.

You have never really prayed until you've learned to wait, and to wait with release. Abandon yourself—let God change the king's heart. This is tough; it cuts across the grain of our human nature. But stand firmly. Give up your own homemade solutions and run the risk of letting God take charge.

3. Faith Is Not a Synonym for Disorder or a Substitute for Careful Planning.

People of faith need orderly minds. Leaders like Nehemiah think through the problems they face. Although their circumstances may allow them to go only half a step now, you can be sure they have already thought through the next twelve. Why? Because faith breeds organization—they go together.

A few years ago I had the opportunity of working with businessmen, and it was one of the best learning experiences I have ever had. For more than three years, I met regularly with a group of salesmen associated with a large corporation. During those encounters I learned to think a lot more like businessmen think, and I learned to appreciate them.

Almost everything that is presented to businessmen is communicated in terms of practical facts. These facts form the foundation upon which further discussion is built. From these committed Christian businessmen, I learned that God honors orderly thinking. He isn't pleased when we expect Him to spare us the pain of failure when we haven't even considered the cost of success. Of course, He does not want us to fail in that to which He calls us, but He is pleased when we plan.

4. Opposition Is to Be Expected When God's Will Is Carried Out.

When a person knows he is following God's will, it is unusual if there is not at least one person who opposes him. I have rarely known it to be otherwise.

Don't you love this guy Nehemiah? He meets us right where we live. When he faced financial needs, he asked the king for letters. When he was afraid, he said, "Lord, give me the words to say." He was a man of faith, yet he carefully balanced faith with realism. He didn't have to have a detailed game plan in his hands, but he thought through the expected difficulties. He was a man of indomitable courage. Think of how he left all that he knew in Susa, got on his mount and took off—on an eight-hundred-mile journey. What a great experience! Yet, how threatening—how risky from a human viewpoint.

Nehemiah has displayed four prerequisite steps to be taken by those who would desire to discover and develop their leadership potential and skills. He (1) realized his own limitations—only God can change a man's heart; (2) turned to God—praying and waiting; (3) organized a feasible plan of action (while waiting for the Lord to answer); and (4) pressed on, despite vocal opposition, to execute the plan—once God opened the way.

A plan is primary; waiting for God to work is essential; but following through with people is where it's at. In the next chapter we will move into the phase where the rubber of leadership meets the road of reality—the whole issue of stimulating and motivating others to roll up their sleeves and get the job done.

4

Getting Off Dead Center

Studying Nehemiah's story is a little like listening to a concerto. Just as a musical concerto features a soloist, this literary concerto features Nehemiah. He was not the director; God was the Director. The soloist, however, played his instrument with beautiful technique.

A concerto employs a major theme or melody. The main theme of the Book of Nehemiah is *leadership*. There are counterparts such as planning, prayer, opposition, and government; but in spite of the secondary melodies, the basic theme of leadership comes through over and over again.

Finally, every concerto has at least three major movements, and often each one is played in contrast to the others. One may be quiet and soft; the next, passionate and stirring; and the last may have a touch of all the others, closing with a climactic crescendo.

The same is true in Nehemiah's story of leadership. The first movement takes place from chapter 1 through chapter 2, verse 10, and in it we see Nehemiah playing his part as the king's *cupbearer*. Beginning at verse 11 of chapter 2 to the end of chapter 6, there is the soul-stirring second movement of Nehemiah as the *builder*. The final movement of the book commences when we reach chapter 7 and proceed—in one great crescendo—to the end of the book. In these last five chapters we see Nehemiah as the *governor*.

If I could press the analogy just a bit further, I'd say that in no other movement does the soloist display greater technique or brilliance than in the second. When Nehemiah became a builder, determined to construct the wall around Jerusalem, I feel he became one of history's great leaders. However, his role as builder didn't begin very eloquently. The first movement ends after having built to a thundering climax in verse 11. You can almost hear the roll of the percussion, the blare of the horns, and the harmony of motion among the strings as Nehemiah proclaims, "I came to Jerusalem."

It is at this point that Nehemiah behaved quite differently from what we might expect. The hurried reader would think that Nehemiah, having reached his destination, would be driven by an inner burning compulsion to pull out the trowel, hire subcontractors, and hang the plumb line; in short, to get someone started on the wall—*fast!* But, he didn't do that. As a matter of fact, *he didn't do anything.* The concerto's second movement begins in the latter part of verse 11 with Nehemiah's statement, ". . . and [I] was there three days."

Why didn't he immediately go to work? Because he didn't know what God had for him. As a matter of fact, God was silent.

Now, I don't know if it took place during those three days or right after them, but notice what happened next: "I arose in the night, I and a few men with me. I did not tell any one" (v. 12). In verse 16, Nehemiah reported further: "The officials did not know where I had gone or what I had done; nor had I as yet told the Jews, the priests, the nobles, the officials, or the rest who did the work."

It is this side of leadership that the uninvolved observer or even the workers never see. People have the false idea that a leader lives an exciting life in the limelight, basking in the experience of one ecstatic public applause after another. That image of a successful leader is promoted throughout the nation by exposure on television and in the press, or through internal communication channels within a company. But God begins this account of Nehemiah's second role by showing us that successful leaders know how to handle themselves in solitude.

It's in silence that a person secures the respect of the public. Right now as a nation we are aching in our political veins. For some of us it's the first time we have wondered about what is really happening in the solitude of the Oval Office. We have been raised to trust our national leaders. We hate to ask those hard suspicious-sounding questions because we long to respect our leaders' hidden actions. Unfortunately, that sense of unquestioned trust has faded.

Before Activity . . . Meaningful Solitude

If you think that being extremely busy equates itself with spirituality, learn a lesson from Nehemiah. It is not in the rush and the hurry of activity that a person gains the respect of those around him; it is what he does when he is all alone. Someone once aptly penned, "Character is what you are when nobody's looking."

What was happening, during Nehemiah's silent days? Nehemiah 2:12, tells us: "I did not tell any one what my God was putting into my mind." In that small, apparently insignificant phrase, there are volumes of knowledge. In the time of quietness when there was no activity, God was putting into Nehemiah's heart some top-priority information.

If you're a Sunday school teacher or pastor, you minister to others by teaching God's Word. But are you a student of the Word? Are you taking special note of what God has written?

Every once in a while a young man interested in being a pastor will ask me about the secret of a successful ministry, as if there were some clever behind-the-scenes maneuvering involved. My answer is usually to the point: Do your homework. Be what you ought to be when nobody's looking. Do the job; and do it to the very best of your ability for the sheer joy of glorifying God in the process. And that requires time in the Scripture!

That was a major secret of Nehemiah's success. He was faithful behind the scenes. He listened to the Lord.

While searching God's mind, Nehemiah received some objective direction.

So I went out at night by the Valley Gate in the direction of the Dragon's Well and on to the Refuse Gate, inspecting the walls [notice that]. . . . Then I passed on to the Fountain Gate (vv. 13,14).

He went on down through the southern part of Jerusalem and back up the west side to the Fountain Gate. When Nehemiah came to the King's Pool, it was such a mess he couldn't even get by on his horse. He undoubtedly got off and walked along ahead of the mount. And he wrote: "[I] went up at night by the ravine and inspected the wall." Twice he talks about inspecting the damage (vv. 13–15). The Hebrew word for *inspect* means "to look into something very carefully." It's a medical word for probing a wound to see the extent of the damage.

Nehemiah made a careful, conscious, probing examination of the wall for one reason: As leader, it was his job to be aware of the details and to develop a plan of action. But there is a vast difference between being *aware* of the details and being *lost* in those details. The individual who is able to stand back—being fully aware of the facts and yet not lost in them—is the one best equipped to lead.

Nehemiah made a careful investigation of the facts. In his mind, he was developing a master plan for the whole process of construction and determining the necessary personnel and building materials.

As Nehemiah was inspecting gates and walls and other sections of the city, he might have thought to himself, "Now, let's see. Who will be able to do this job best? That section will require a craftsman in this trade. Digging would not have to be done by skilled craftsmen. Pulling weeds and moving the old rubble—pushing it aside to make way—well, anyone can handle that."

In other words, Nehemiah planned it all out. He knew the job must fit the individual. All the groundwork for the gigantic undertaking was taking place in the silence and solitude of this time.

After Solitude . . . Strong Motivation

Nehemiah had done all his homework and made all his inspections. He was finally ready to discuss the need of rebuilding the city wall. It was time to get off dead center: "Then I said to them . . ."

Nehemiah did not say anything about his plans for three days. After that, he stood in front of the city council and said, "You see the bad situation we are in, that Jerusalem is desolate and its gates burned by fire. Come, let us rebuild the wall of Jerusalem that we may no longer be a reproach" (v. 17).

In my Bible, I've circled three vitally important words in verse 17: *we, us,* and *we.* In order for him to motivate the city planning commission and potential employees, he had to identify himself with the need.

Imagine the kind of response he would have received if he had said, "You folks have gotten yourselves into a bad mess. You know what you need to do? You need to rebuild that wall. If you need me, I'll be in my office. After all, I wasn't part of the problem. You people will have to get it on and do the work!"

When you cast blame and criticism, you squelch motivation. When you identify with the problem, you encourage motivation.

But even though Nehemiah identified with the people and was personally concerned about the problem, he did not try to hide the hard facts. He did not plead or threaten; nor was he negative in his approach. He simply said, "We've got to do something about this problem. Let's rebuild the wall." Nehemiah extended the invitation to rebuild the wall and gave the people a reason for accepting it: "That we may no longer be a reproach."

There are two kinds of motivation: *extrinsic motivation,* which is the most common but used by fewer great leaders, and *intrinsic motivation,* which appeals to the internal part of a person.

Consider the use of extrinsic motivation. You say to your child, "Come on, honey, it's time to get your bath. It's Saturday night . . . bath night. Let's clean up."

And the child answers, "I don't want to."

You respond, "I'll let you watch TV if you hurry."

That's an example of external incentive.

When the child gets a little older and starts to school he is told by his parents, "For every 'A' you make, we'll give you a dollar." When that same child enters college, he is told, "If you make good grades, you'll get on the dean's list." Again, that's extrinsic motivation. In the business community, there is the "Christmas bonus" or "special trip to Hawaii" that may be earned by increasing sales volume. That's scratching people where they itch—externally.

Extrinsic motivation appeals to our materialistic attitudes. However, not all external or extrinsic motivation is wrong. Occasionally, it is the thing that does the trick, especially with children or among those who need to be rewarded for a job well done. But it is not the best way to get people to see the value of their energy investment.

Nehemiah did not promise any material incentives when he addressed the Jerusalem officials. He didn't offer prizes to the fastest-working families or a week at the Dead Sea for the group doing the most attractive work. He didn't stoop to that kind of motivation—but many churches do. We give children prizes for bringing their friends to church, memorizing Bible verses, or having a perfect attendance record. That might work with kids for awhile, but something is wrong when it has to continue. As we grow older, intrinsic motivation should have greater appeal. Nehemiah simply said, "See the ruins? We're in a terrible strait. Let's rebuild this wall." And the people said, "Let's do it."

Why did the citizens respond in willingness to Nehemiah's proposal? Being led by God, Nehemiah was able to appeal to their *intrinsic* zeal. He was able to scratch them where they itched deep inside. There aren't many people who can do that today; there never have been. But they make the best leaders.

I just finished reading a biography of Winston Churchill. I have always been impressed with the story of that man. In Churchill's speeches, I cannot find a time in which he ever employed extrinsic motivation. Listen to his words:

> I have nothing to offer but blood, toil, tears, and sweat.
>
> Victory at all costs, victory in spite of all terror, victory however long and hard the road may be; for without victory there is no survival.
>
> We shall not flag or fail. We shall go on to the end. We shall fight in France, we shall fight in the seas and oceans, we shall fight with growing confidence and growing strength in the air; we shall defend our Island whatever the cost may be.
>
> We shall fight on the beaches, we shall fight on the landing grounds, we shall fight in the fields and in the streets, we shall fight in the hills; we shall never surrender.[6]

He said to our president on February 9, 1941, during a radio broadcast: "Give us the tools, and we will finish the job."[7]

And I will never forget the amazing speech he gave to a very fearful people in Britain when he addressed the House of Commons on December 30, 1941. It included these words:

> When I warned [the French] that Britain would fight on alone whatever they did, their generals told their Prime Minister and his divided Cabinet, "In three weeks England will have her neck wrung like a chicken." Some chicken; some neck.[8]

The Nazis never wrung England's neck. Somehow Churchill, stubby little creature that he was, could stand in front of a microphone and strengthen Britons by the thousands with intrinsic motivation. He appealed to their zeal.

I'm reminded of David when he put off the armor of Saul and looked into the face of that ugly giant across the valley. He said, "Is there not a cause?" And while everybody else stood around figuring the odds, David shouted, "Get out of the way!" He picked up a few rocks, and you know the rest of the story. David possessed that marvelous inner motivation to never surrender. It was that same inner strength and commitment that Nehemiah communicated:

> I told them how the hand of my God had been favorable to me. . . . Then they said, "Let us arise and build." [And what did they do?] So they put their hands to the good work (v. 18).

Someone once suggested, "If you really want to check the leadership of an individual, just see if anybody's following him." It was at this point that Nehemiah emerged as a leader. His new followers said, "Let's build. Let's put our hands to the good work."

With Motivation . . . Inevitable Opposition

Notice that right away opposition comes! It never fails. There is direct criticism of the plan. As soon as the rebuilding crews rolled up their sleeves, they were opposed. Murphy's Law could again be heard: "But when Sanballat the Horonite, and Tobiah the Ammonite official, and Geshem the Arab heard it, they mocked us and despised us" (v. 19).

The Hebrew term for *mock* means "to stammer," "to stutter," "to utter repeatedly words of derision." Sanballat and Tobiah held their heads high, looked down their noses, and scoffed at that little group of Jews, saying, "You're out of your minds. You'll never be able to do it. After all, you're rebelling against the king, aren't you?"

I can see Nehemiah once again whip out those letters! "Here are the words of the king," he yelled. "I have Artaxerxes' okay."

But he did more than that. Nehemiah issued a get-tough policy at just the right time.

> So I answered them and said to them, "The God of heaven will give us success; therefore we His servants will arise and build, but you have no portion, right, or memorial in Jerusalem" (v. 20).

Nehemiah knew that he and the people of Jerusalem were doing God's work, and he was not going to listen to anyone actively opposed to what he knew was right. And furthermore, he did not intend to associate with those who would seek to stop what was obviously of God. He was determined to allow no one but God to stop the work.

I wonder how many of us would have said, "You know, people really don't want a new wall. We can't go on with this project because the opposition is too vocal. They haven't had a wall here in more than 150 years now, and they've gotten used to living like this. There's just no use changing. Let's pack up and pull out."

Nehemiah, however, planted his feet firmly and held to his original position.

Part of the unwritten job requirements for every leader is the ability to handle criticism. That's part of the leadership package. If you never get criticized, chances are you aren't getting anything done. A wise leader will evaluate the opposition in light of the spirit and attitude in which criticism is given. He will also consider the voice to which the opposition listens. If your critics listen to

God's voice, you had better listen to them. But if they are marching to a different drumbeat, use the Nehemiah technique: "Look, they're not even in the same camp. Let's go right on."

And you know something? Those stubborn men who opposed Nehemiah's mission still didn't leave. They stayed around until the entire wall was built! When it was halfway finished, they taunted, "A little old fox could knock down that wall." But remember, they were now outside the wall shouting over it.

As Nehemiah led the others in building the wall, he had his eyes on the baton of the Director.

Do you realize you can have your eyes in various directions in the Christian life? You can have your eyes glued on *some other person.* If you do, before long you will be disappointed or even disillusioned because that person will fail. Never set your eyes on some church staff member or church officer or another friend. That's the best way I know of crippling your walk. Instead, steady your focus on God.

You can have your eyes on your own situation and become absorbed in self-pity, or you can get your eyes on *yourself* and be puffed with pride or demoralized by insecurity. With your eyes on yourself, you are constantly comparing your life with someone else's. You will never stay balanced while fighting the comparison battle.

The choice is yours. You can permit your eyes to wander aimlessly, or you can simply look up and fix your eyes on the *Director.* Though you might have what you call an insignificant part in the total orchestration, you will never miss your cue.

5
Knocked Down, But Not Knocked Out

No leader is exempt from criticism, and his humility will nowhere be seen more clearly than in the manner in which he accepts and reacts to it.[9]

Anyone who steps into the arena of leadership must be prepared to pay a price. True leadership exacts a heavy toll on the whole person—and the more effective the leadership, the higher the price! The leader must soon face the fact that he will be the target of critical darts. Unpleasant though it may sound, you haven't really led until you have become familiar with the stinging barbs of the critic. Good leaders must have thick skin.

We left Nehemiah on the dart board at the close of the last chapter. It was intentional. Knowing that his critics were not through, I chose to deal with them at length in this chapter, rather than attempt a brief and hurried analysis earlier. However, before we delve into the growing problem of opposition faced by Nehemiah, let's look at an unusual promise found in 2 Corinthians 4.

Anyone who is serious about serving God as a leader in the church of Jesus Christ should make a serious study of Paul the apostle. Paul's life is something of a pattern that people in leadership should follow. Second Corinthians is a key book for study because he talks more about himself in this book than in any of his others.

We should not be surprised to read an honest admission about the toll of the ministry in Paul's life in 2 Corinthians 4:7: "But we have this treasure in earthen vessels, that the surpassing greatness of the power may be of God and not from ourselves." "We have this treasure in earthen vessels" refers to an earthenware jar, a clay pot. He was describing the treasure of the gospel, saying that it is housed in a clay jar, meaning our humanity. "We have this treasure [the gospel] in earthen vessels [our frail human bodies] that the surpassing greatness of the power may be of God and not from ourselves." There is no power or strength in a clay pot. It is fragile and ugly. It often leaks. The passing of time only makes the vessel weaker. Paul was saying that any manifestation of power comes not from the pot, but rather from what the pot contains.

Next, Paul described what the life of a pot was like:

> We are afflicted in every way, but not crushed; perplexed, but not despairing; persecuted, but not forsaken; struck down, but not destroyed; always carrying about in the body the dying of Jesus, that the life of Jesus also may be manifested in our body (2 Cor. 4:8–10).

Always is the key word in verse 10. Here, Paul described the life of the spiritual leader as "always carrying about in the body the dying of Jesus." The marks of death are always on the lives of people God uses most.

These marks of death are evident in the lives of God's leaders because God wants to display the life of Jesus in the pot. You see, God is interested not only in blessing that which is in the pot but also in using the pot itself. God doesn't declare abstract truth from the lips of an angel; He puts truth in real life. Then He brings that life before people, whether it is in business, a Bible class, a group of disciples, a growing Christian school, a mission organization, or a church. He uses imperfect people—clay pots—to display the glory of God. It is also emphasized in this passage that opposition is inevitable. A godly leader always carries about the telltale marks of death.

I love the way J. B. Phillips puts the same verse together in his *Letters to Young Churches*. He writes:

> We are handicapped on all sides, but we are never frustrated; we are puzzled, but never in despair. We are persecuted, but we never have to stand it alone: we may be knocked down but we are never knocked out![10]

The Presence Of Opposition

As we look again at Nehemiah, keep in mind that for the leader opposition is inevitable. Nehemiah had one task, and that was to build a wall around the city of Jerusalem. It doesn't sound very spiritual, but it was God's will for his life.

In the process of that task, Nehemiah was led by God to appoint workmen for various parts of the project. Some were to build certain gates; some, a section of the wall. Some were to build in the south; others, up north of the city. But everybody had a job to do. The delegation of labor is described in elaborate detail in chapter 3 of the Book of Nehemiah.

Shortly thereafter, we read about the opposition that Nehemiah faced while the wall was being built. *God's will didn't allow the wall to be built without opposition.* It was before the wall was half finished that the workers began to be bombarded with the sarcastic words of the critics: "Now it came about that when Sanballat heard that we were rebuilding the wall, he became furious" (4:1). What prompted the opposition was the progress in the construction project. One would think that seeing this small band of people succeeding in a massive project would evoke admiration. But this was not so. You see, the heart of the habitual critic resists change. To him, change is a threat. In any organization, those who are most critical of change are those who are most inflexible. They resist change, and they become especially suspicious of changes that lead to progress and growth.

It was the change—the growth—that incited Sanballat's anger. Notice also the others involved in the opposition. Sanballat heard about rebuilding the wall in verse 1. "He spoke in the presence of his brothers and the wealthy men of Samaria" (v. 2); and "Tobiah the Ammonite was near him" (v. 3). I point this out to emphasize something that is usually true: *Critics run with critics.*

And obviously while not all criticism is of the devil, this criticism was. It was destructive and disturbing.

Every leader must develop the ability to measure the value or worth of criticism. He has to determine the source and the motive, and he has to listen with discernment. Sometimes the best course of action is to repond to criticism and learn from it. Other times, it must be completely ignored.

Nehemiah's critics were constantly with one another and their reaction was not a quiet, mildly disinterested one. No, they were angry! They became sarcastic. Look at the sarcasm in verse 3. It makes one chuckle. "Now Tobiah the Ammonite was near him [Sanballat] and he said, "Even what they are building—if a fox should jump on it, he would break their stone wall down!"

Can you imagine a comment like that? But Tobiah made a crucial mistake. He claimed that a mere fox "would break their stone wall down." That was not "their" stone wall. *God designed the wall.* He happened to use Nehemiah as the superintendent, but the Designer was God. Just as Jesus said, "I will build My church; and the gates of Hades shall not overpower it." (Matt. 16:18), so the wall would be built because God desired for it to be. Critics constantly look at situations from a human point of view—*their* walls, *their* plans, *their* procedure, *their* arrangement. They don't stop to think that they may be criticizing God's project.

Just like Nehemiah's critics, today's world is so mesmerized with "splash," "size," and "tangible security" that it cannot fathom God's doing an impossible thing among an insignificant bunch of people.

People who look at life from the human point of view have problems with projects that require giant steps of faith. We as Christians need to say to ourselves, "Am I really looking to God for vision, for growth, and for direction, or am I sitting back and saying, 'Oh, let's just maintain?'" We who would seek God's best for our lives must learn to keep our eyes open and our attitudes positive—not lacking in discernment, but positive. And we must never forget there will always, *always* be opposition from those who are, by nature, negative and critical. But the work must go on. Progress should not stop because a few are critical of the plan. Remember that!

Facing Criticism Squarely

Nehemiah was faced with opposition—those sidewalk supervisors who would have had him discontinue building the Jerusalem wall. He did two significant things in response to the criticism: He prayed and he persisted.

First, in verses 4 and 5, *he talked to God about the criticism.* He prayed: "Hear, O our God, how we are despised!" The next part of the prayer may surprise you because it is rather unusual.

> Return their reproach on their own heads and give them up for plunder in a land of captivity. Do not forgive their iniquity.

Would you look at that? It's rare! The Bible is filled with "forgive our iniquities," "forgive us of our sins," "relieve us of our transgressions," "cover over our transgressions"; but Nehemiah said, "*Don't* forgive their iniquities"; "Let not their sin be blotted out before Thee, for they have demoralized the builders."

Nehemiah fought his battles through prayer. We have seen it numerous times in his life. Through the therapeutic process of time on his knees, he laid out his concerns before God. It is common knowledge that the first thing most leaders will do when attacked is retaliate. Leaders are often people of very strong wills. It took a get-tough mind-set to build a wall around Jerusalem and to face opposition like this. It would have been quite human for Nehemiah to punch out their lights. But he didn't.

Remember what David said before he took the stone and sling in hand with which to slay the Philistine giant Goliath? He said, "For the battle is the Lord's and He will give you into our hands"

— 67 —

(1 Sam. 17:47). That must have sounded rather strange to Goliath. Here was this little tiny runt coming toward him with a sling, mumbling something about the battle being the Lord's. It put him down, and Goliath must have wondered, "What kind of fellow is this?" Then all of a sudden it was over—smack! He was hit right between the running lights! Goliath was defeated. The Lord won His battle.

Take a glimpse of Daniel, who when commanded to worship the image of Nebuchadnezzar didn't say, "Let me at him!" Instead, Daniel slipped upstairs to his room and, as he had done at previous times, fell before the Father and prayed.

You are never more successful than when you are on your knees in prayer. The saint who advances on his knees need never retreat because prayer provides an invincible shield! "A gentle answer turns away wrath, but a harsh word stirs up anger" (Prov. 15:1). What do we do when a harsh word is spoken to us? We usually shout louder. The recent argument in your home lasted as long as it did because one of you kept yelling. Arguments are never a one-way street. They run in twos; sometimes in packs. If you want to stop an argument, close your mouth. The other person will usually just run down. If you want to keep the argument going, answer the complaint or criticism in a harsh way. Look at verses 28 and 29 in the same chapter of Proverbs:

> The heart of the righteous ponders how to answer [Lord,
> how should I answer this situation? You have to find that
> out through prayer.]
> But the mouth of the wicked pours out evil things.
> The Lord is far from the wicked.
> But He hears the prayer of the righteous.

If you want wisdom in knowing how to handle any problem, drop to your knees. James 1:5 says if you need wisdom, ask God for it.

Before Nehemiah ever said a word to the critic, he talked with God. He refused to retaliate even though others might have encouraged him to do so.

One of the knottiest situations a pastor can put himself into is personal retaliation. He is going to be criticized by some, no matter what. The worst thing he can do is fight every critic, one by one.

When I was serving the Lord in a church in Waltham, Massachusetts, there was a church in the same area that had an amazing history. One of its pastors inherited a terrible mess when he first went to the church. Attendance was down, and those who did attend sat in the back three pews. On this pastor's first Sunday there he picked up the pulpit and literally carried it down the aisle, placing it near the people. I was told that Sunday after Sunday he kept having to move the pulpit back toward the front of the sanctuary until finally he was almost perched in the choir loft! Ultimately, the place was filled each Sunday morning. He preached the Word, walked with God, and faithfully labored in spite of opposition. Eventually, God chose to call him to a school that has consistently moved ahead under his guidance.

He was followed by a retaliatory man, a fighter. This man held several graduate degrees; he was brilliant. He had traveled and was an experienced leader of people. He seemingly possessed a lot more experience and brains than the first fellow. Like his predecessor, this pastor experienced criticism and hostility on the part of certain segments of the church membership; and week by week, through one public argument and retaliatory action after another, the church systematically emptied. Sure, he won the arguments, but he lost the battle. Both pastors were criticized, but what a difference in their responses! One man fought on his knees, the other on his feet.

The very first thing that ought to result from criticism is prayer. This principle should be applied in business, at home, and at school, as well as at church. Never am I used of God more significantly than when I am praying for my critics.

The Need For Common Sense

Nehemiah approached opposition in two ways. First, he took his setbacks to God in prayer; and second, *he stayed at the task*. He persisted. I love what Nehemiah wrote in chapter 4, verse 6: "So we built the wall." I can just feel it. "Keep mixing the mortar and hand me another brick!"

So we built the wall and the whole wall was joined together to half its height, for the people had a mind to work.

Critics demoralize. Leaders encourage. When the critics spoke, the workmen heard them and were demoralized. But when the capable leader stepped up and said, "Let's look at it God's way; stay with the job," the crew members were back in there with those trowels and wheelbarrows, putting together the stone and the mortar, the gates and the hinges.

Nothing excites Satan or the critic more than for his negativism to result in a slowdown of progress. The easiest thing to do when one is criticized is to give up.

Nehemiah said, "Stay at the task. Don't give up. Keep building." You could hear the workmen day and night, splashing on that mortar, putting the stones into place. That productive activity should have assaulted the hearts of Sanballat, Tobiah, and Geshem—but that's not the case. In fact, the size of their group grew. Verses 7 and 8 tell us that Sanballat and Tobiah were joined by the Ammonites and the Ashodites; and they even added some Arabs! They intensified the opposition. And when they

> heard that the repair of the walls of Jerusalem went on, and that the breaches began to be closed, they were very angry. . . . they conspired together to come and fight against Jerusalem and to cause a disturbance in it.

There are times when criticism doesn't die down—*it intensifies.* Not only did the critics expand their troops, but they also added an intensity in the opposition. They planned a conspiracy and arranged to cause a disturbance.

What did Nehemiah do when confronted with continued harassment? As was his custom, he intensified his prayer: "But we prayed to our God, and because of them we set up a guard against them day and night" (4:9). The intensified opposition might have knocked him down, but it was a long way from knocking him out.

Intensified opposition against the will of God calls for an intensified response. Nehemiah not only heard the opposition, but he also analyzed available data, prayed, and took decisive, practical action. He said, "Let's set up a guard against them." That was a common-sense response. He persisted by taking up arms.

Occasionally, persistence in the form of common sense must prevail. Do you fear that someone is going to break into your home? Certainly, you should trust God, but don't forget to lock the doors. Don't just pray about it. It is foolish to leave doors unlocked when you are praying that your home will not be burglarized.

Out of a job? Pray! But hit the road too. Fill out the résumé. Make contacts. Get in touch with as many opportunities as possible. The Lord doesn't have any trouble hitting a moving target. In fact, it's easier to steer a moving vehicle than one that is immobile.

We will read more about Nehemiah's common sense in the next chapter, but before we do I don't want us to miss three very practical truths that can be gleaned from Nehemiah 4.

1. *It is impossible to lead anyone without facing opposition.* The leader must learn to take the heat. He will face opposition—it's an occupational hazard of every leader. Darts *will* be thrown.

2. *It is essential to face opposition in prayer.* The first response to opposition *must* be prayer. Prayer is the single, most-often-overlooked discipline in the Christian life among leaders.

3. *Prayer is not* all *that is necessary if opposition grows.* That was true of David. He prayed when Saul was after him, but he also ran like mad! When opposition intensified, he ran faster. When it got worse, he hid in more obscure places. In most cases, the critic isn't worth the worry. But if the leader has prayed and yet finds himself facing intensified opposition, common sense must be employed.

A number of months ago I became discouraged because of criticism. My optimism eroded as a lengthy chain of events led me into "the pits." Knowing of my need for encouragement, my wife searched for a way to lift my spirits. She found a hand-lettered statement written by a statesman I have always admired, used it to make a wooden decoupage plaque, and gave it to me as a gift. What an encouragement it is! I often read it when opposition abounds and my shoulders start to droop—when I am knocked down and feel like I am about to be knocked out. It reads:

It is not the critic who counts: not the man who points out how the strong man stumbled or where the doer of deeds could have done them better. The credit belongs to the man who is actually in the arena; whose face is marred by dust and sweat and blood; who strives valiantly; who errs, and comes short again and again, because there is no effort without error and shortcoming; who does actually try to do the deed; who knows the great enthusiasm, the great devotion and spends himself in a worthy cause; who, at the worst, if he fails, at least fails while daring greatly.

Far better it is to dare mighty things, to win glorious triumphs even though checkered by failure, than to rank with those poor spirits who neither enjoy nor suffer much because they live in the gray twilight that knows neither victory nor defeat.[11]

I repeat the opening statement of this chapter: No leader is exempt from criticism. Don't expect to be. But when it comes, be ready to battle against discouragement, which is poised and ready to strike on the heels of criticism. You can count on it!

6
Discouragement: Its Cause and Cure

A funny thing happened in Darlington, Maryland, several years ago. Edith, a mother of eight, was coming home from a neighbor's house one Saturday afternoon. As she walked into the house, she saw five of her youngest children huddled together, concentrating with intense interest on something. As she slipped near them, trying to discover the center of attention, she couldn't believe her eyes. Smack dab in the middle of the circle were several baby skunks. She screamed at the top of her voice, "Children, run!" *Each kid grabbed a skunk and ran!*

When I first read that true story in John Haggai's *How to Win Over Worry,*[12] I thought of Nehemiah. Like that mother, he had no idea how complicated life could get. He took on a project that had all the appearance of being harmless, innocent, and rather simple. After all, what could be very difficult about building a wall around a city? It seemed that Nehemiah would be able to have that wall completed in just a few weeks; then he would go back to Persia and take up where he left off. But not so!

He looked over the shoulders of those workmen, and it was like suddenly confronting a living room full of skunks! In fact, the more he tried to alleviate the problem, the greater it became. First there was sarcasm. Then there was mockery, which led to open opposition, criticism, and finally conspiracy. The conspiracy was so great that before long the inevitable took place—discouragement set in. No matter how hard he tried, Nehemiah was unable to correct the problems. They just got worse; they multiplied and magnified as time went on. Finally, as he shouted, "Keep building!" each workman grabbed a skunk and ran!

I suppose all of us, in some measure, have experienced a situation like Edith's or Nehemiah's. While trying to solve a problem, it got worse right before our eyes.

The problem that plagued Nehemiah was that of discouragement. What a difficult disease to cure! I don't know of anything that will take the wind out of your sails quite so quickly as discouragement. Rare is the person who can resist it.

I was reading recently a brief but stimulating biography of Thomas Edison written by his son. What an amazing character! Thanks to his genius, today we enjoy the microphone, the phonograph, the incandescent light, the storage battery, talking movies, and more than a thousand other inventions. But above and beyond all that, he was a man who refused to be discouraged. His contagious optimism affected all those around him.

His son recalled a freezing December night in 1914. It was at a time when still unfruitful experiments on the nickel-iron-alkaline storage battery, to which his dad had devoted almost ten years, had put Edison on a financial tightrope. The only reason he was still solvent was the profit from the movie and record production.

On that December evening the cry of "Fire!" echoed through the plant. Spontaneous combustion had broken out in the film room. Within minutes all the packing compounds, celluloid for records and film, and other flammable goods were in flames. Fire companies from eight surrounding towns arrived, but the heat was so intense and the water pressure so low that the attempt to douse the flames was futile. Everything was destroyed.

When he couldn't find his father, the son became concerned. Was he safe? With all his assets going up in a *whoosh*, would his spirit be broken? After all, he was 67—no age to start all over. Then—in the distance—young Edison saw his father in the plant yard running toward him.

"Where's Mom?" shouted the inventor. "Go get her, Son! Tell her to hurry up and bring her friends! They'll never see a fire like this again!"

Early the next morning, long before dawn, with the fire barely under control, Edison called his employees together and made an incredible announcement: "We're rebuilding!"

He told one man to lease all the machine shops in the area. He told another to obtain a wrecking crane from the Erie Railroad Company. Then, almost as an afterthought, he added, "Oh, by the way. Anybody know where we can get some money?"

Later he explained, "We can always make capital out of disaster. We've just cleared out a bunch of old rubbish. We'll build bigger and better on the ruins." Shortly after that he yawned, rolled up his coat for a pillow, curled up on a table, and immediately fell asleep.[13]

Nehemiah, like Edison, faced insurmountable odds, but he refused to be annihilated by discouragement.

Source of Discouragement

Before we consider either the causes or the cures for this ailment, notice the source of Nehemiah's problem—the people of Judah (see Neh. 4:10). Way back in the last chapters of Genesis, we discover that Judah was not just *any* tribe among the people of Israel. Judah was the leader.

In Genesis 49, we read that Jacob summoned his sons before him and cast upon them blessings, warnings, predictions, and discouragements. When he came to Judah (see v. 8) he said, "You're going to be a leader among the family. Your brothers will praise you." Then he added, "The scepter shall not depart from Judah, nor the ruler's staff from between his feet until Shiloh comes" (v. 10). Imagine the word *Shiloh* to mean "Messiah": "Judah, you will be the Messianic tribe. Through your tribe there will some day be born the Savior of the world, the Messiah. The scepter will never depart from you. And to Him (that is, to Shiloh) shall be the obedience of the peoples." These people of Judah were to be re· spected because they were the chosen ones through whom the Lord Jesus would some day be born.

But when you get to Nehemiah 4, you find that it is Judah, of all people, who is bringing the words of discouragement to the troops. Not only were they coming from Judah, but verse 12 tells us of another source of discouragement: "It came about when the

Jews who lived near them . . ." These Jews lived near the enemy, the ones who said in verse 11, "We . . . [will] kill them, and put a stop to the work." They kept hearing those threats day after day. In fact, we read in verse 12 that these Jews came and warned Nehemiah ten times of the dangers of continuing. It was just a matter of time, they claimed, before the Jews would be wiped off the earth.

It's important to note that the discouraging information came from people who lived "near" it. *You cannot constantly hear negativism without having some of it rub off on you.* If you are prone to discouragement, you can't run the risk of spending a lot of your time with people who traffic in discouraging information.

Nehemiah's discouragement came first from Judah, which was very surprising, and next from those Jews who lived near the critics—which was very significant.

Causes of Discouragement

If we look closely, we will discover four causes for Nehemiah's discouragement.

1. A Loss of Strength

Verse 10 reads, "Thus in Judah it was said, 'The strength of the burden bearers is failing.'"

See the word *failing?* The original text says "stumbling," "tottering," "staggering."

"These people, Nehemiah, have been working a long time, and they are getting tired."

How long had they been building this wall? Verse 6 tells us they were halfway through:

"The whole wall was joined together to half its height." The newness had worn off.

Let me make it even more practical. Have you ever bought a new car? Can you remember when it lost its newness? Probably when you got halfway through paying for it.

Let's say you have undertaken a difficult project of redecorating your home. When is the most discouraging time? Usually it's when you are halfway through and the mess gets to be more than you can handle.

Maybe you've tried mountain climbing. You look up and say, "Oh, maybe an hour—an hour and thirty minutes at the most." Five hours later, when you're halfway up, you look back down and say, "I think the Lord is leading us back!"

Halfway is discouraging!

"We're getting tired, Nehemiah. The strength of these who have been working is failing." A loss of strength takes an emotional toll on our bodies.

2. A Loss of Vision

Did you notice what Judah said? "Yet there is much rubbish" (4:10). The word *yet* is significant because it connects the thought with the previous statement. The burden bearers' strength was expended and began to fail; *yet,* in spite of all the work, there's a lot of rubbish. The Hebrew word for *rubbish* means "dry earth," "debris."

"We look around, Nehemiah, and all we can see is debris—dirt, broken stones, hard, dried chunks of mortar. It's getting tiring. There's too much rubbish."

Rubbish and discouragement are Siamese twins.

The builders had lost the vision of the completed wall. A perfect illustration of this myopic outlook is the young mother who has changed what seems to be fifty or sixty diapers in one day. She looks at the situation and says, "There's too much rubbish, too much mess, too many diapers, too much work." What has she lost? She has lost the vision of that growing child and the delight of introducing her son or daughter to society. She has lost her whole sense of fulfillment in the motherhood role because of the current "rubbish."

Some of you are involved in jobs right now that are very demanding—even threatening—and there are difficult people to work with. Or maybe the tasks seem endless. You can easily begin to lose the whole vision of your work because of the "rubbish" surrounding you.

3. A Loss of Confidence

Perhaps the most devastating cause of discouragement is an obvious loss of confidence. Nehemiah's workers became weary and disillusioned. The wall was halfway up. Rubbish was strewn everywhere. They voiced their feelings by sadly observing, "We ourselves are unable to rebuild the wall" (v. 10). When you lose strength and you lose vision, then you lose confidence. And when you've lost confidence, discouragement is winking at you around the corner.

These Jews had built the wall to half its height because the people "had a mind to work." The Hebrew reads, ". . . the people had a heart to work." But now *they lost their heart.* When you lose your confidence, you lose your heart; you lose your motivation. A number of things can cause that, but there is always an empty feeling—that overwhelming, discouraging sense that you are never going to catch up.

4. A Loss of Security

The final cause for discouragement in the case of these Jews was a loss of their feelings of security. Verse 11 reads, "And our enemies said, 'They will not know or see until we come among them, kill them, and put a stop to the work.'" What a scare tactic!

The enemy said, "We've got a plan. No, we're not going to tell anybody what the plan is; but, when you least expect it, *wham!* We'll slip in and that will be it. We will handle the job so fast and so thoroughly that you'll never know we were even there."

The laborers suddenly slumped into discouragement when they lost their security.

There are many areas of life that we hang onto for tangible security. One area is our jobs. If all your security is wrapped up in your job, then all you need to do is lose that job, and discouragement will swamp you.

Another familiar security blanket is close friends and familiar circumstances. A move to some other part of the country threatens that. Let's say, for example, that your husband comes home to-

— 78 —

morrow afternoon and says, "Honey, the company wants to move us to Bangor, Maine."

"Bangor, Maine? What in the world is in Bangor, Maine?"

Everything you know and love surrounds your current location. You've never been beyond your secure backyard. Your whole lifestyle is determined by your long-time residence where you now live. Your "roots" are being loosened. All the tangibles that you've hung onto for security are threatened. In an instant, discouragement can come. Your sense of security has been shattered!

You might think that discouragement is only for those not walking with God. That's not true. Some Christian leaders admit that occasionally times of discouragement have been signals from God announcing a whole new direction and plan. Strange though it may seem, discouragement, brought on by a removal of our tangible securities, has been known to usher in incredible achievements.

Such was the admission of Charles Haddon Spurgeon, one of the greatest spokesmen for Christ that English-speaking people ever heard. Here is his own admission:

> Before any great achievement, some measure of depression is very usual. . . . Such was my experience when I first became a pastor in London. My success appalled me, and the thought of the career which seemed to open up, so far from elating me, cast me into the lowest depth, out of which I uttered my miserere and found no room for a gloria in excelsis. Who was I that I should continue to lead so great a multitude? I would betake me to my village obscurity, or emigrate to America and find a solitary nest in the backwoods where I might be sufficient for the things that were demanded of me. It was just then the curtain was rising on my life-work, . . . This depression comes over me whenever the Lord is preparing a larger blessing for my ministry.[14]

Have you ever wanted to run away? What a desire we have to escape, to get away from life's demands. But after enduring the discouragement we could be led to an opportunity offering unbelievable fulfillment.

Maybe you are standing before the door of opportunity or change. You've lost your strength. You've lost your confidence.

You've lost your vision. And you've lost your security. There's that feeling deep down within you that says, "It isn't worth it.'" But wait! You could be on the verge of the greatest years of your entire life.

How Can We Deal with Discouragement?

Building that Jerusalem wall was certainly turning out to be no easy feat! Discouragement ran rampant. Satan must have been having a field day. But Nehemiah didn't ignore the discouragement. (You can't ignore discouragement. It's like ignoring a flat tire. Pray all you want to; drive all you want to; you never will get air back into it. You've got to fix it. That's the way it is with discouragement.)

Nehemiah rolled up his sleeves like a good leader and dealt with the discouragement. I find five techniques he employed that worked for him and will still work today.

1. Unify Your Efforts Toward a Goal

The first thing Nehemiah did was unify the people around the same goal.

> I stationed men in the lowest parts of the space behind the wall, the exposed places, and I stationed the people in families with their swords, spears, and bows (Neh. 4:13).

Now that is significant. The builders have been scattered all over Jerusalem working together with stones, water, and mortar, and yet *separated from their families*. Nehemiah unified them according to families and gave each one a common goal—preservation. He turned their attention from themselves to the enemy, from the discouragement of self-pity to the goal of self-preservation. He "tightened the ranks" and thereby encouraged the disheartened.

The home should be a basic source of encouragement. Nehemiah's work force was discouraged. He said, "Come on, let's get together according to families. You folks sit here; you and your family are stationed there. . . ." Nehemiah brought them together as units.

Notice what happened in the process of uniting his people: Nehemiah *stopped the work.* Sometimes the very best thing to do when you are discouraged is to take some time off. There's an old Greek motto that says, "You will break the bow if you keep it always bent." How tight is your bow? When is the last time you loosened the bow and got away for a couple of days?

I suppose we all get up tight and tense in our work, but workaholics don't make the best leaders. I'll say it again: Take time off once in awhile!

Nehemiah stopped the work and said, "Let's pull together as families." That will do a lot to stop discouragement.

2. Direct Your Attention to the Lord

Next, he directed their attention to the Lord (v. 14). They were looking at the rubbish. They needed to be looking to the Lord.

> When I saw their fear, I rose and spoke . . . "Do not be afraid of them; remember the Lord who is great and awesome. . . ."

Look at that. He took charge. That's a basic job of the leader! The phrase, "Remember the Lord," sounds good, but how do you do it? You can begin by *calling to mind the things the Lord has said.* You actually put in your mind some of the statements God has made. For example,

> The steadfast of mind Thou wilt keep in perfect peace,
> Because he trusts in Thee.
> Trust in the Lord forever (Isa. 26:3,4).

Or,

> Be anxious for nothing, but in everything by prayer and supplication with thanksgiving let your requests be made known to God. And the peace of God, which surpasses all comprehension, shall guard your hearts and your minds in Christ Jesus (Phil. 4:6,7).

— 81 —

You remember the Lord by remembering what the Lord has said. Call to mind right now five or six good, solid promises that you could claim. When the devil attacks, are you ready with the living words that shoot back—the sword of the Spirit, God's Word? The Christian must know what God has said.

You can remember the Lord by *calling to mind who He is*. When is the last time you reflected upon the greatness of God? Perhaps it was while lying flat on your back, looking up at the stars. Do you ever get in your car and drive to a secluded spot just to find some quiet time alone with God? That often helps clear away the fog and enables the mind to renew its grip on God's character. Equally essential are those occasions when Christians feast at the Lord's Table. Communion is God's "show and tell" time, revealing anew the wonder of His Person.

Nehemiah said to his people, "You've got your eyes on the rubbish, the debris, your own individual project. Get your eyes on the Lord." People who are discouraged are thinking mainly about one thing—*themselves*. Those people were no exception.

So Nehemiah unified them around the same goal. That means he had to stop the work process and get them alone. Then he turned their attention to the Lord.

3. Maintain a Balance in Your Thoughts and Actions

What did Nehemiah do next in his attempt to thwart discouragement? He encouraged the Jews to maintain a balance. He called them to action. "Now, you've got to fight," he commanded. "There's a job to be done. Draw swords!" Verse 14 concludes, "Fight for your brothers, yours sons, your daughters, your wives, and your houses." Look at verses 15 and 16:

> And it happened when our enemies heard that it was known to us, and that God had frustrated their plan, then all of us returned to the wall, each one to his work. And it came about from that day on, that half of my servants carried on the work while half of them held the spears, the shields, the bows, and the breastplates.

Verse 17 adds, "Those who were rebuilding the wall and those who carried burdens took their load with one hand doing the work and the other holding a weapon."

That, my friend, is a basic fact of the Christian life. I'm really weary of Christians who do nothing but fight, but of equal concern is the Christian who says there is never a reason to fight. I heartily agree with a balanced philosophy of life that encourages both building and battle.

You and I have an English Bible in our possession largely because of a man named John Wycliffe. He was known not only as a builder, producing the first English text of the Bible, but also as a fighter. What a leader! His enemies burned him at the stake and took the ashes of his body and sprinkled them over the Thames River in London. "Forever, we're rid of Wycliffe!" his enemies must have thought. They were wrong. The product of his labors—the English Bible—is with us today because he did more than fight. He stayed at the task.

Remember John Bunyan—fighter and builder. They threw him into prison three times, thinking that would silence him. Instead he penned *The Pilgrim's Progress,* the second most-loved book among Christians today. You see, he could do more than fight. By his making a gigantic personal investment, the truths of *The Pilgrim's Progress* were expounded for the benefit of millions in subsequent generations. What a beautiful balance!

Guard against the subtle teaching that suggests that God does everything and you step back and do nothing. The Bible continually exhorts us to stand, to contend for the faith, to be strong in the fight, and to be good soldiers. But we must balance faith with action.

4. Determine a Rallying Point

The fourth thing that Nehemiah did was to provide a rallying point. Let me clarify what I mean. Nehemiah wrote in verse 19, "And I said to the nobles, the officials, and the rest of the people, 'The work is great and extensive, and we are separated on the wall far from one another.'" Now in verse 20 we read of the rallying point: "At whatever place you hear the sound of the trumpet, rally to us there. Our God will fight for us."

What was the rallying point? First of all, it was a *place*, but it also suggests a *principle*. The place was wherever the sound of the trumpet was coming from. Nehemiah ordered, "Whenever you hear that trumpet sound, you come running to the spot where the bugler is standing." The principle: Don't try to fight alone.

The principle is still true; we need a rallying point. We need a close friend, somebody we can attach ourselves to whenever the attack comes. Don't try to fight it alone. None of us should say, "I don't need anybody else." That's poor theology and conveys a warped idea of Christianity. The response of the healthy child of God is, "I can't possibly do it alone. But, O God, if You will give me Your strength through Your Spirit and link me with a brother or sister in the family who can encourage me and whom I can encourage, I will be rallying around You until the last day of that test."

Is there any Scripture that supports the need for a rallying point? Indeed there is! When Elijah was being hunted down by Jezebel, he ran under a tree in the wilderness and said, "Lord, take my life. It's not worth it. I'm all alone." What did God do? He brought in food, and Elijah was nourished and sustained by that food forty days and forty nights.

The next thing you know, God was saying, "Elijah, get up. You're not alone, Elijah." And He gave Elijah a companion named Elisha. The last verse of 1 Kings 19 says that Elisha ministered to Elijah. The beautiful part of this story is that this happening marked the time when Elijah really began to make tracks. He had found a rallying point. God gave him a buddy with whom he could be accountable (that's extremely important), bare his soul, share his hurts, and relieve his loneliness.

When David was under Saul's jealous scrutiny, God gave David a friend. Jonathan and David loved each other because of a marvelous bond; their souls were linked together as one. Discouragement seldom weakened David's armor because of that friend.

Do you have somebody like that? If not, cultivate someone. Look for, long for, pray for such a friend. Don't give up until you can link your soul with another who has a kindred spirit, who cares for your soul and for your needs. You need someone to be your rallying point. Nehemiah said, "When you hear the battle cry, come to where the trumpet is." That's where strength is.

5. Develop a "Serving Others" Ministry

The fifth and final thing that Nehemiah did to dispel all signs of discouragement among his people was to occupy them in a ministry of serving others. Verses 21 and 22 tell us that they carried on the work.

> So we carried on the work with half of them holding spears from dawn until the stars appeared. At that time I also said to the people, "Let each man with his servant spend the night within Jerusalem so that they may be a guard for us by night and a laborer by day."

In essence, Nehemiah was saying, "Hey, we need help. I'm asking you to serve and assist each other. We can't handle it alone." In the pressured days that followed, according to verse 23, they didn't even have time to change clothes! When they went down to the water to bathe, they stayed at the task. They ministered to one another in service and involvement.

Do you want to know how to be miserable? Be like the late Howard Hughes; live only for yourself. Use *I*, *me*, and *my* as often as possible. Turn all your love inward. Think only about your own needs, your desires, your wants, your pleasures. Refuse to love and be loved.

C. S. Lewis said it best:

> To love at all is to be vulnerable. Love anything, and your heart will certainly be wrung and possibly be broken. If you want to make sure of keeping it intact, you must give your heart to no one, not even to an animal. Wrap it carefully round with hobbies and little luxuries; avoid all entanglements; lock it up safe in the casket or coffin of your selfishness. But in that casket—safe, dark, motionless, airless—it will change. It will not be broken; it will become unbreakable, impenetrable, irredeemable. . . . The only place outside Heaven where you can be perfectly safe from all the dangers . . . of love is Hell.[15]

How involved are you in others' lives? This week, how much of your life will be spent serving others? Or is it all wrapped up in yourself? Everyone of us should take a long look at our short lives, taking special note of our personal investment in the lives of others.

Do you want to know how not to feel useless after you retire? Stay in touch with the needs of others. Recently, an older member of our congregation died. One of the girls in our office said to me, "The heartbreak is that her breed is dying."

This sweet lady lost her husband in 1946, and since that time she had been one of the busiest ladies I knew. Her volunteer help was invaluable to our church and the community. Even in the twilight years of her life, she could be found working as a volunteer for the cancer society, working in the ladies' auxiliary, doing civic work, helping out at the local hospital—the list went on and on. She was involved in others' lives. And she *never* got old. I never saw her discouraged!

Retirement in America means, "Don't bother me. I've no time for others." I suggest an alternative. Just think of the ministry of encouragement God could give you when He releases you (through retirement) from the work-a-day world and uses you as a servant.

Nehemiah said, "Let's not sit around and lick our own wounds. We need help from one another. Let's get at the business of caring. Let's serve. Let's minister."

Isn't that what the raw edge of Christianity is all about? Am I not to give up my rights and say no to myself?

Discouragement is indeed an internal disease. It starts with the germs of self-doubt. Through fear and negative exaggerations, the germs begin to grow and multiply. Soon we lose our way, we weaken, and we run and hide. As it continues, we become virtually useless and downright defeated. We become easy prey for the enemy of our souls to take charge and nullify our efforts. It can happen almost overnight.

Glance back over the five techniques Nehemiah used to combat the "blahs" in the camp at ancient Jerusalem. His methods will never be outdated.

Discouragement may be tough to handle, but it's certainly not impossible. Remember, it is not a terminal disease.

7

Love, Loans . . . and the Money Crunch

Making sense with dollars is a basic task of any leader. Very few projects are accomplished without an outlay of cash. And when cash starts to flow, wisdom, honesty, self-control, and intelligent, realistic planning must prevail.

Even Jesus addressed the importance of financial planning.

"But don't begin until you count the cost. For who would begin construction of a building without first getting estimates and then checking to see if he has enough money to pay the bills? Otherwise he might complete only the foundation before running out of funds. And then how everyone would laugh! 'See that fellow there?' they would mock. 'He started that building and ran out of money before it was finished'" (Luke 14:28–30, TLB).

To our Lord, careful money management is not considered an optional luxury. It is an essential ingredient in the lives of those in leadership.

Since the Book of Nehemiah illustrates nearly every major principle of leadership, we shouldn't be surprised to find Nehemiah facing the money issue. We read of this in the fifth chapter of his book and it seems so typical you will think he is living in twentieth-century America.

A strike occurred among the laborers who had been building the Jerusalem wall. They probably didn't picket the site by carrying hand-painted signs and blocking traffic, but they stopped working and started bad-mouthing their conditions: "Now there was a great outcry of the people and of their wives against their Jewish brothers" (5:1).

"We've gone on strike!" they might have said. "It isn't fair. We have our rights!" They temporarily halted construction to voice their grievances.

Nehemiah, like a good leader, sized up the situation as he listened to their gripes:

- Some had large families without enough to eat (see v. 2).
- Others owned property, yet had to mortgage their homes and property to endure the spiraling inflation problem (see v. 3).
- Still others were heavily in debt, unable to pay back what they owed (see vv. 4,5).

It was a miserable, panic-ridden situation. How could that have happened?

Reasons For The Crunch

If we look carefully, we discover three reasons for the complaints in these same five verses.

1. There was a *famine*. Verse 3 reads, "We are mortgaging our fields, our vineyards, and our houses that we might get grain because of the famine."

Why was there a problem? The city had not been tilled and cultivated to meet the demands of the hundreds of people who suddenly flooded into it to build the wall. The existing limited crop could not sustain them. Add to the increased demand for food the fact that the whole area was experiencing a famine, apparently caused by a drought.

2. There were *too many taxes* exacted from them by Artaxerxes. Verse 4 reads, "We have borrowed money, for the king's tax on our fields, and our vineyards."

You see, Artaxerxes controlled the known world at that time. Taxes were collected from all who lived in the kingdom, and these laborers, even though they lived eight hundred miles from Persia, were not exempt. It is also possible that those collecting the taxes exploited the taxpayers by demanding more than the tax called for.

3. The *high and inappropriate interest rate* caused them to sell their children and themselves into slavery. Read verse 5:

> "And now our flesh is like the flesh of our brothers, our children like their children . . . we are forcing our sons and daughters to be slaves, and some of our daughters are forced into bondage already, and we are helpless because our fields and vineyards belong to others."

Their creditors were taking their land as payment and when they ran out of land, the creditors took their children as slaves. So the work on the wall ground to a halt.

Is the Bible outdated? Does it sound like a book that's irrelevant? It speaks here of overpopulation, famine, and high taxes. Interest rates were higher than ever with no relief in sight. There were inequities and strikes. Verses 1 through 5 read like today's *Wall Street Journal*.

Look at the leader's reaction in verse 6: "Then I was very angry when I had heard their outcry and these words." Nehemiah heard them griping and complaining. When he saw they had stopped the job they were called to do, he was infuriated!

When All Else Fails, Read the Instructions

Why was Nehemiah angry when he heard their outcry? Should not a leader be given to compassion when people complain? At times he should, but not always. Sometimes the very best response is justified anger.

Nehemiah was angry because the people had forgotten the Mosaic Law. Today we are living in the era of grace and so we look disparagingly (unfortunately) on the law. We shouldn't. It preserved the people of Israel by telling them how to live with one another. God's tribes were to live differently from others because of His personalized instructions to them. His law gave the Jews instructions for living a just and godly life as a family. But the chosen ones were having problems in Nehemiah's day because they had failed to follow instructions.

Twentieth-century Christians would also do well to pay close attention to God's guidelines. Notice the instructions in Exodus 22:25: "If you lend money to My people, to the poor among you, you are not to act as a creditor to him; you shall not charge him interest." Notice that God says this has to do with "My" people, the Jews. "If you find one in a poor financial situation," God continues, "don't act as a creditor. When you lend, lend *without* interest."

Now, look at Deuteronomy 23, verses 19 and 20:

> You shall not charge interest to your countrymen: interest on money, food, or anything that may be loaned at interest. You may charge interest to a foreigner [a non-Jew], but to your countryman you shall not charge interest.

Why does God give those explicit instructions to potential creditors? Verse 20 continues: "So that the Lord your God may bless you in all that you undertake." God was saying that He wanted His people, the Jews, to be unique. In effect, He was saying, "I will bless you, and you won't have to charge interest to your own brothers. You will maintain a distinction that will cause the foreigner to rub his bearded chin and say, 'How in the world can that nation continue?' And you can answer, 'The Lord, our God provides our needs without interest among ourselves.' That will make you distinct. Then the Lord your God will bless you in all that you undertake."

In between Exodus and Deuteronomy is a passage in Leviticus 25 that may also have been in Nehemiah's mind.

> Now in case a countryman of yours [a fellow Jew] becomes poor and his means with regard to you falter, then you are to sustain him like a stranger or a sojourner, that he may live with you. Do not take usurious interest from him, but revere your God, that your countryman may live with you. You shall not give him your silver at interest, nor your food for gain. [Don't give him one bushel of grain, expecting one and a half back. Give him one for one.] I am the Lord your God, who brought you out of the land of Egypt to

give you the land of Canaan and to be your God. And if a countryman of yours becomes so poor with regard to you that he sells himself to you, you shall not subject him to a slave's service. He shall be with you as a hired man, as if he were a sojourner with you (vv. 35–40).

No Jew was ever to enslave another Jew. Such action was evidence of an absence of love and concern for his brother. Their family love was to supersede love of money. God's instructions (which they willfully disobeyed) would have protected and preserved the Jews of Nehemiah's day during this period of stress. But because they chose their own problem-solving method, they sank into the quicksand of increasing compromise.

We know by Nehemiah's reaction to the people's complaints that he knew these four principles found in the Law:

- It is not wrong to lend money to a non-Jew for interest.
- It is not wrong to lend money to a Jew.
- It *is* wrong to demand interest on a loan to a Jew.
- It *is* wrong to enslave a fellow Jew.

Nehemiah got angry because the people knowingly ignored and disobeyed God's Word. That's a pretty good reason to get angry! Righteous indignation is appropriate. When God's beautiful pattern is violated, something is wrong if we don't feel uneasy. It's difficult to maintain a sweet spirit when you see individuals misusing their tongues, conducting their lives immorally, or ignoring direct counsel from the Book of books.

Solving The Dilemma

Now, look at the next verse. I love this: "And I consulted with myself" (v. 7). Aren't you glad that's in there? Yes, he got mad, but he thought before he spoke. In those moments of self-consultation, God was able to speak to Nehemiah about what to say next. Self-control is a virtue the leader cannot afford to be without.

Nehemiah, when very angry, found a way to cool down. He consulted with himself and listened to God's voice. The Hebrew word for *consult,* as used here, means "to give one self-advice," "to counsel oneself." That's the very best thing to do when you get mad. You need to have a quiet place where you can lay all the emotions of your soul before God. Nobody hears but God. Marvelous therapy comes from sharing with God the hurt and the anger as you "consult with yourself" before you face the situation head-on.

Now, we're ready to look at the solution to Nehemiah's problem: "And I consulted with myself, and contended with the nobles and the rulers." Why did he speak to the ruling elite? They were the men with the money, the ones who were exacting interest from those who didn't have it. They were responsible for the oppression of the laborers.

I appreciate the fact that Nehemiah didn't penalize everybody. He went to the primary source of the problem, those who were responsible. Nehemiah called before him the guys with the heavy wallets. He lined them up in front of him and confronted them with the fact of their violations.

Nehemiah made three accusations. Mark each one carefully:

- You are charging interest to fellow Jews. That is wrong (see v. 7).
- You are enforcing the permanent slavery of the Jews (see v. 8). That's also wrong.
- You are losing your distinction in the eyes of the surrounding nations. That is tragic!

    The thing which you are doing is not good; should you not walk in the fear of our God because of the reproach of the nations, our enemies? (v. 9).

"You guys are over here making a bundle," Nehemiah implied, "and those guys (the Gentiles) across the way are looking on, saying, 'They're just like everybody else—no different at all; in fact, the whole project is a joke.'" Nothing could have thrilled Sanballat and his crowd any more than to see the job stopped because of internal strife.

Do you know who applauds the loudest when churches split?

Those who don't know Christ. They say, "Ah, I knew it would happen. I knew if those so-called Christians had enough time, they'd cut their own throats."

After Nehemiah rebuked the ruling elite, notice their beautiful response: "Then they were silent and could not find a word to say" (v. 8). That is the very best response when you are under deep conviction.

A good leader, however, does not stop with rebuke. Nehemiah took steps to correct the problem. The same steps can be taken by us to deal with sin in our own lives.

1. *Determine to stop it.* Look at verse 10: "Let us leave off this usury [the interest]." People occasionally ask me what they should do when convicted of sin. The answer is simple: Make plans to stop it! Willfully decide to eliminate the wrongdoing, right now. You cannot gradually stop sinning.

2. *Make specific plans to correct the situation as quickly as possible.* Nehemiah confronted the bankers:

> Please, give back to them this very day [look how quick he is—*right now*] their fields, their vineyards, their olive groves, and their houses, also . . . [the interest] the grain, the new wine, and the oil that you are exacting from them (v. 11).

When God shows us a particular sin that we are guilty of, He doesn't tell us to take our time dealing with it. No, He says, "Deal with it NOW!" When we realize what we are doing wrong, *now* is the time to stop it. Making long-range plans to correct a problem allows the sands of time to hone off the raw edges of God's reproof in our lives. We end up tolerating that sin and perhaps even protecting it. Such laxity greatly concerns our Lord. A prompt and thorough dealing with wrong in our lives is essential. As in finances, it is best to keep all accounts current.

3. *Declare your plans for correction in a promise before God.* Verse 12 reads, "So I called the priests and took an oath from them that they would do according to this promise."

Look at that! Nehemiah called the priests in—the men who represented the Jews to God. Pointing to the money-lenders, he said, "You men make a promise to these men over here. And you men (the priests) remember this before God." It was a public hearing, a public declaration, and a public promise before God. Nehemiah knew how to come to grips with an issue!

4. *Realize the serious nature of your vow to God.*

> I also shook out the front of my garment and said, "Thus may God shake out every man from his house and from his possessions who does not fulfill this promise" (v. 13).

If there's ever a time to take God seriously, it's when we make a promise to Him.

A high school buddy of mine in east Houston was just as mean and coarse and ornery as he could possibly be. A member of the football team, he was a fullback on offense and middle linebacker on defense. He was a wild rebel and tough as a boot! He owned a speed boat and loved to zing around the shores of Galveston full speed ahead (preferably in the middle of the night). Late one night, going full speed, he hit a shallow reef and flipped the boat. He was in a mess, for a storm blew in, and the only thing he had to hang onto was a barnacled rock. The waves buffeted him up and down against those razor-like barnacles for several hours. Blood from his wounded body began to spread out into the water and he was terrified that sharks would be drawn to him. He fervently prayed, "Oh, God, if You will please deliver me from this, I'll serve You for the rest of my life. I'll make my life right. I'll do anything!" He vowed, "I'll even be a *preacher*" (the ultimate sacrifice, he felt). God, in His marvelous grace, dispatched the Coast Guard, and they picked him up.

A week later he had forgotten all about his vow. His body eventually healed and he was back at his old tricks again. He told me later that every time he took off his shirt, the scars that stretched across his chest and abdomen were mute reminders of his promise to God. He just put them out of his mind. He would shower and towel off, quickly turning his back to the mirror because those scars haunted him with the thought, "You made God a promise."

Several months later, my friend was involved in a head-on collision. It was a miracle he wasn't killed. He now bears a terrible scar across his face and neck along with those on his body. He lost part of the use of one of his arms, and some of his organs were impaired. But, guess what he is doing today? He's preaching the gospel, scars and all. He says, "Every time I shave, I'm reminded that promises to God are to be taken seriously." A vow is nothing to shrug off as insignificant.

Once the Jews came to terms with what God had said, they were able to praise the Lord (v. 13). *Shalom* returned, along with happiness, the sounds of construction, and God's special favor.

But What About Today?

You may be asking, "What does all this in Nehemiah 5 say to me today? First of all, let me remind you: *God is pleased when we handle our money wisely.*

Many Christians are excellent in areas of public ministry, but in the handling of their money, they're a reproach to the name of Christ. Through what we have seen in Nehemiah's experience, it is clear that proper money management is important to God. The way we earn it, save it, invest it, spend it—and, of course, *give* it. Does God get His proper amount? Some may give ten percent of their income; for others, it should be fifteen to twenty-five percent. It amazes me when a Christian thinks he or she can live without a well-thought-through plan for giving, since the Lord emphasized the importance of financial faithfulness so clearly and repeatedly in His Book. Wise handling of our savings, our investing, our spending, and our giving pleases our God. Never think that money doesn't matter to your Master.

There's something else to remember: *Prolonged personal sins take a heavy toll on God's work in your life.* This excludes no one. Dr. Clarence Macartney, a great pastor for many years in Pittsburgh, addressed this issue as it relates to the pastor's responsibility to live obediently before the Lord:

> The better the man, the better the preacher. When he kneels by the bed of the dying or when he mounts the pulpit stairs, then every self-denial he has made, every Christian forbearance he has shown, every resistance to sin and temptation, will come back to him to strengthen his arm and give conviction to his voice. Likewise every

evasion of duty, every indulgence of self, every compromise with evil, every unworthy thought, word, or deed, will be there at the head of the pulpit stairs to meet the minister on Sunday morning, to take the light from his eye, the power from his blow, the ring from his voice, and the joy from his heart.[16]

Sin follows you around like your shadow. If there's sin in your life, get rid of it! Lay it out before God, or get out of the ministry! Be man enough to step aside until you are a clean vessel.

Notice that in the first thirteen verses of Nehemiah 5 there is no mention of the wall. No building was going on. One cannot build while on a spiritual strike; instead, the miserable status quo is maintained.

I observe another timeless lesson: *Correcting any problem begins by facing it head-on.* Some of us are pros at avoiding the truth. Because it is painful to confront sin in our lives, we dodge it. We excuse it. In essence, we don't want to endure the pain of reality—and so we hide behind the famous cop-out: "Oh well, nobody's perfect. You know, that's just the way I am. Always have been—always will be." Who says? God is a specialist in the business of changing lives. Claim the power of the indwelling Holy Spirit and say, "God, take over. Change my attitude. I'm sick of this habit. It is sin."

"Well, you know, I'm given to being angry. I just get mad easily. My dad had a temper; so do I."

Take care of it! Come to severe terms with that sin!

"Well, I'm given to drink. You know how it is. Man, I have trouble. I go on a binge about every third weekend."

Deal with it! Do whatever it takes to correct it.

"I'm given to gossip. It's always been hard for me to control my tongue. But that's the way I am. But so are a lot of people. Just a little problem I live with."

It's SIN! Painful and long and expensive as the process may be, you cannot afford to skirt the issue any longer. Face it head-on.

The final thing I discover in this chapter of Nehemiah's journal is: *Correction is carried out most effectively when we make a promise, preferably a public promise.* Confess your sin to someone who knows you well and share how you plan to deal with it; or—

if God leads you—publicly share your problem and solution with your discipleship group or close circle of friends. One major step toward the correction of wrong in our lives is by being accountable to a close personal friend. Or make your vow to God known to your family. Nail it down. Lay it before someone. If you don't, operation erosion will set it.

Back in 1958 a small community in northeastern Pennsylvania built a little red brick building that was to be their police department, their fire department, and their city hall. They were proud of that building; it was a result of sacrificial giving and careful planning. When the building was completed, they had a ribbon-cutting ceremony, and more than six thousand people were there—nearly all the town's residents. It was the biggest event of the year!

Within less than two months, however, they began to notice some ominous cracks on the side of this red brick building. Sometime later, it was noticed that the windows would not shut all the way. Then it was discovered the doors wouldn't close correctly. Eventually, the floor shifted and left ugly gaps in the floor covering and corners. The roof began to leak. Within a few more months, the building had to be evacuated, to the embarrassment of the builder and the disgust of the taxpayers.

A firm did an analysis shortly thereafter and found that the blasts from a nearby mining area were slowly but effectively destroying the building. Imperceptibly, down beneath the foundation, there were small shifts and changes taking place that caused the whole foundation to crack. You couldn't feel it or even see it from the surface, but quietly and down deep there was a weakening. A city official finally had to write across the door of that building, "Condemned. Not fit for public use." Ultimately, the building had to be demolished.

When I read the account several years ago, it occurred to me that a similar erosion process affected not only Saul's life and Solomon's life and the lives of others in Scripture but also the lives of people today. F. B. Meyer once said, "No man suddenly becomes base." It is a quiet and lengthy process. Erosion goes on unnoticed.

Perhaps you are involved right now in the beginning of foundational cracks. The windows of finance in your life are not closing too well. The doors of discipline have been left ajar. The floor of integrity is starting to crack. It is easy to rationalize the truth and to ignore the painful realities of compromise. You may slap on a heavy coat of cover-up paint after filling in the cracks with lots of putty, but before long all you will be is an empty shell, a miserable mask of phony veneer.

There is a better way. It calls for absolute honesty and a refusal to excuse or ignore reality any longer. It means being sensitive and obedient to the Father's instructions. It requires personal appropriation of those things mentioned in the last part of this chapter—starting today.

8
How to Handle
a Promotion

Adversity is a painful teacher. Who hasn't felt its
sting? It can be the heartache of unhappy employment or the discouragement of losing a job. It can suddenly reduce your status, force you into selling your home, or
make you start over in another occupation that has no frills or
thrills. Even worse, adversity can mean having to stand in line for
an unemployment check.

In Southern California the space industry once provided thousands of people a taste of "the good life." With the moon and a
half dozen planets to explore, with space shuttles to build, with a
seemingly endless supply of federal funds and an ever-increasing
number of government contracts, it looked as though we were
dreaming our way into a financial millennium. The dream, however, became a nightmare.

Almost overnight the space projects were shelved. Contracts
were withdrawn. Pink slips replaced work orders. Executives—
some with more than twenty years of seniority—were released. It
was not uncommon to see Ph.D.'s pumping gas and doing yard
work. Men and women, highly educated and uniquely skilled, suddenly found themselves demoted and disillusioned. Adversity had
struck again. Like a cancer, its plundering invasion robbed the
victim of all motivation and hope. Some of us who lived through
those terrible days will never forget them.

But there's a test that's even worse than adversity: *advancement.*

That sounds wrong, but it's right! As Thomas Carlyle, the Scottish essayist and historian, once declared, "Adversity is hard on a man; but for one man who can stand prosperity, there are a hundred that will stand adversity."[17]

Few people can live in the lap of luxury and maintain their spiritual, emotional, and moral equilibrium. Sudden elevation often disturbs balance, which leads to pride and a sense of self-sufficiency—and then, a fall. It's ironic, but more of us can hang tough through a demotion than through a promotion. And it is at this level a godly leader shows himself or herself strong. The right kind of leaders, when promoted, know how to handle the honor.

A fellow named Asaph was the type of man Carlyle described— "one in a hundred." We don't know much about him except that he wrote twelve of the Bible's psalms. Of the twelve, there is one— Psalm 75—that convinces me that Asaph had his head and heart together.

Sandwiched between the first and last sections of the psalm, three verses (5–7) flash like a neon sign, announcing wise counsel for anyone with a new promotion:

> 'Do not lift up your horn on high,
> Do not speak with insolent pride.'
> For not from the east, nor from the west,
> Nor from the desert comes exaltation;
> But God is the Judge;
> He puts down one, and exalts another.

Asaph said something like this: "Don't toot your own horn! Remember, your promotion didn't just evolve. Behind your recent exaltation was the sovereign hand of God. You are the recipient of His goodness and grace."

Is that ever easy to forget! And your non-Christian friends won't see it like that, believe me. To them, a promotion comes by being in the right place at the right time, by knowing the right person, by shaking the right hands, by favoring the right boss, by scratching the right back.

That's just not so. God is the One who suddenly lifted Joseph from an Egyptian dungeon to the role of prime minister. Almost overnight He exalted Daniel from a Babylonian boot camp to the king's right hand. He's the One who promoted Amos, an ignorant figpicker, to the polished, sophisticated halls of Bethel to be His personal spokesman. God knew that Joseph, Daniel, and Amos could handle a promotion.

And so could Nehemiah. Nehemiah provides one of the best biblical illustrations on how to handle a promotion. We've already seen how balanced he was. He worked to handle situations when things were bad, and he stood firm when things were good. Nehemiah rolled on when the project was moving ahead; and he paused and relaxed when the project briefly came to a halt. He knew *when* to requisition more bricks. He was a competent leader, and as a result, he was promoted.

The Art Of Acceptance

Nehemiah writes in chapter 5, verse 14:

> From the day that I was appointed to be their governor [that was the *highest position*] in the land of Judah, from the twentieth year to the thirty-second year of King Artaxerxes.

What was Nehemiah's reaction to his appointment? Quite frankly, it can be said in one word: *acceptance.* Many Christians seem afraid to accept responsibilities that are beyond themselves. For example, how many Christians can you name who stand firm as uncompromising believers in places of political power? It is not because Christians are unqualified that there are so few. Some of the most qualified people I know are born-again people. But frequently we Christians adopt the idea that to be spiritual one must hide in the shadows, but you have to be carnal to live in the limelight. Not so!

We all need to be more like Jabez, an little-known fellow we find tucked away in 1 Chronicles 4. He had the courage to pray (verse 10): "Oh that Thou wouldst bless me indeed, and enlarge my border, and that Thy hand might be with me, and that Thou wouldst keep me from harm, that it may not pain me!"

In other words, Jabez did not say, "Lord, give me some tiny spot where I can spend the rest of my days in obscurity." No, he looked to God and said he was willing to accept "enlarged borders." We need to believe that God wants to use us in "stretching" experiences.

If you tend to set your goals far lower than God does, you need the encouragement of Proverbs 29:2:

> When the righteous increase, the people rejoice,
> But when a wicked man rules, people groan.

"When the righteous increase. . . ." The Hebrew word for *increase* means "to be made great"; a synonym would be "promoted." So, Proverbs 29:2 might be read,

> When the righteous are promoted, the people rejoice,
> But when a wicked man rules, the people groan.

Regardless of the perils of leadership and promotion, I hope you will never forget Proverbs 29:2. In this proverb, Solomon gave us a tremendous truth. When born-again people are promoted to places of increased leadership in their companies, they will have underneath them individuals who rejoice because of their "righteous" rule. How much better is this than to have the wicked promoted, who would bring with them all the tentacles of corruption and compromise.

Nehemiah accepted his appointment. Our prayer should be that God will raise up more Christians in strategic spots: college professors, university presidents, business executives, film makers, artists, governors, senators, and others who can fashion and frame the minds of the public. There are already some Christians in these roles, but not nearly enough.

Nehemiah accepted the governorship and immediately was faced with four major concerns that confront anyone who accepts a promotion. All four are found between verses 14 and 18 of chapter 5.

Promotions Bring Privileges

First of all, *with every promotion there are privileges.* New or added rights, benefits, and special favors are provided. The wise leader will use them without abusing them. Nehemiah said (v. 14) that for those twelve years "neither I nor my kinsmen had eaten the governor's food allowance." Not once did Nehemiah take advantage of the food privileges that were his to enjoy. As governor, he had a food allowance for official entertaining. However, he didn't take liberty with his expense account. The food was at his fingertips, but he never lost control.

How does this relate to the practicalities of today? Suppose you have been promoted in your company. With your promotion may have come the privilege of an unlimited expense account. A child of God, who is a person of integrity, will guard against taking advantage of that privilege.

The private life of the promoted leader is under the constant attack of the devil. Many individuals in moving from one economic stratum to the next have been given the privilege of increased privacy. But many of these same people have floundered in their new freedom and slipped down the moral tube. One time when I mentioned this problem in one of my sermons, a successful business executive came to me after the service and said, "Chuck, I want to tell you something. Before my promotion I would have never believed it, but now I recognize how easy it is to fall into the trap of moral compromise. I'm living with it constantly—the attack on my moral integrity." He gave me an illustration. Not long ago on a flight from San Francisco to Los Angeles, he encountered a most appealing temptation, and it came with a perfect built-in excuse for getting involved. After a time of struggling, he refused to yield. He told me, "I live continually with that kind of temptation. I never had such opportunities before my recent promotion. It's easier now that my company trusts me with so much more privacy."

In every promotion there are privileges, but they're not to be taken advantage of. Nehemiah didn't and neither should we.

Let me name another temptation that can come with promotion privileges: the temptation to build one's own empire. It's significant that Nehemiah never started "Nehemiah Enterprises, Incorporated." He didn't establish stock, go public, and then become the largest corporate shareholder. Nehemiah viewed this appointment as governor as a trusted position, and he maintained his integrity. He refused to exploit the privileges entrusted to him.

A biblical illustration demonstrates this point. It's the true account of a man named Absalom who couldn't handle a promotion. Absalom was David's handsome son. He had long, flowing black hair, and was without a blemish from the top of his head to the soles of his feet. He probably never had suffered from pimples and all those other problems that attack one's self-image. He was winsome and had a magnetic personality. He was just a super guy—externally, that is. But, he was *a rebel* at heart.

I believe from a study of Absalom's life that David didn't train him properly. But that wasn't the only reason for his rebellious spirit. He was away from David too much. This great leader separated himself from his son too frequently. And because of guilt over this negligence, David promoted his son to the court. That was a major mistake. Absalom couldn't handle it. Absalom stole the hearts of the people as he sat at the gate of the courts, wanting to be the judge. But because he couldn't handle his new job, he finally overthrew the government and drove his own father from the throne and out of the city.

Handling the temptations of privilege is one of the problems individuals with increased responsibilities have to reckon with. These temptations are one of the reasons that Carlyle said for every hundred who can handle adversity, there's only one who can take prosperity.

Promotions Threaten Policies

We read in Nehemiah 5:15, "But the former governors who were before me [did three things; first of all, they] laid burdens on the people."

That means they overtaxed them. Second, they took payola: They "took from them bread and wine besides [illegally, it seems] forty shekels of silver."

Third, they promoted their servants to a place of domineering leadership. That always seems to be a temptation in the politics of promotion.

When you're promoted, you'll not only have to deal with added privileges, but invariably you will face the pressure of policies. First of all, there will be the former policies. There's something about the old rules that "capture" people. People never seem to realize how great their former manager or boss was *until he's gone.* Suddenly his words are quoted almost as if he were a saint. But those former policies can bring terrible pressure on the new man. That was the case in Nehemiah's time. The problem was a corrupt government; dirty politics was prevalent. Nehemiah came into office and his counselors probably said something like, "You know, Nehemiah, they've been doing it this way all the time."

"Oh? What have they been doing?"

"Well, they get a little extra money from increased taxes here and there. And if you have some buddies who need a job, nobody will squawk. It's part of the system. We've got the perfect setup."

Did Nehemiah adhere to the old way of doing things? Notice his answer in the latter part of verse 15. He only needed five words: "I did not do so." Integrity is what those words reveal. Nehemiah said in effect, "I have a job to do, and I answer to the God of heaven who promoted me. I will not carry on corruption."

An executive began attending our church shortly after I started teaching on Nehemiah. He and his wife were amazed at the relevance of the book. Shortly before this, he had been promoted to a new position with his company. The policies of his predecessor were both unfair and illegal. He had been in the office less than a month when he began a total clean-up campaign. What pressure he endured! His life was threatened more than once, and he and his wife received numerous obscene telephone calls. Ugly and untrue rumors were spread about him. He became a hated man because he refused to allow the former policies to stay in operation. Today the mess has been cleaned up. He has since left the job and accepted another promotion with even a greater measure of authority. Predictably, the man now faces *another* series of similar policies that are requiring radical correction.

This is not unusual. Every person in government, every executive, and every military leader has to wrestle with policies. Constantly they hear, "It has always been done." or "It has never been done." The leader's integrity is at stake. That's why so many people cannot handle the pressures of public office. It's too heavy and they succumb.

Nehemiah said, "I won't do it. I won't succumb to unfair policies, regardless of what has gone on during the last governor's tenure." Nehemiah was like a roast inside a pressure cooker, and his enemies kept the fire on high. Pressure was Nehemiah's constant companion—it came with the job. Unbending (except at the knees!), Nehemiah stood firm. What mattered most to him was where the pressure rested—on him or on the Lord. If he allowed it to come between him and God, he knew he'd succumb. But if it pressed him nearer God's heart, it would be a catalyst.

The privileges? Nehemiah never took advantage of them. The policies? He changed them in the right direction. In fact, it says in chapter 5, verse 16, that Nehemiah applied himself to the brickwork on the wall. He did not buy any land, and all of his servants were "gathered for work." How different from the previous regime! The former governor's servants had been given security and a fat salary. But Nehemiah took office, and being responsible to God he maintained a pure and clean relationship before Him. What a rare man he was. There's not a businessman today who wouldn't agree—someone like Nehemiah *is* a rare man.

Promotions Involve Projects

The third area of concern to a newly promoted employee is what I'll call "the projects." *In every promotion there are projects to be done.* Nehemiah did not take the governorship so he could flit from one of his own enterprises to another. He stayed at the task of building the wall. He did not abuse the promotion. He didn't turn it into a lucrative opportunity for himself. He never lost sight of the goal. Nor did he get sidetracked from the major objective: building the wall.

You might think, "Well, Nehemiah didn't have many problems because he wasn't really very well-known. Governor of Judah? Big deal! After all, he had people like Artaxerxes supporting him politically." If you are questioning his popularity, take a close look at Nehemiah 5:17:

> Moreover, there were at my table one hundred and fifty Jews and officials, besides those who came to us from the nations that were around us.

You may say, "Oh, well, that only happened rarely." Would you believe *every day?* The next verse (v. 18) says, "Now that which was prepared for each day was one ox and six choice sheep, also birds were prepared for me."

The fire in the kitchen stove never went out. He had to feed thousands of people every month. That's a lot of food! Yes, Nehemiah was well-known. He was certainly a sought-after political figure, a very public man. High ranking public officials from surrounding nations were his dinner guests. But Nehemiah never lost sight of the project. His belly didn't block his vision. He maintained a sharp eye that refused to be dulled by people coming and going. Some leaders can do that. Some can't.

Solomon couldn't. He became the richest man who ever lived. From one importing enterprise alone, according to 1 Kings 10, Solomon made the equivalent of $20 million annually. He owned handcrafted shields of solid gold that cost $1800 each. Scripture tells us that under Solomon's leadership the silver in Jerusalem became as common as stones. But Solomon couldn't handle the pressures of responsibility. He lost sight of the primary projects. Listen to this eloquent yet tragic analysis:

> Maddened with the love of show, Solomon swung into a feverish career of wastefulness, impropriety, and oppression. Not satisfied with the necessary buildings and legitimate progress of his past years, he over-burdened his people with taxation, enslaved some, and ruthlessly instigated the murder of others.
>
> All Solomon's drinking vessels were of gold, and those of his house were of pure gold. The shields of his mighty men were made of beaten gold, and his great throne was made of ivory and overlaid with the finest gold. . . . Solomon, like many another absolute monarchs, drove too fast and traveled too far. . . . The monarch became debauched and effeminate; an egotist and cynic, so satiated with the sensual and material affairs of life that he became skeptical of all good—to him, all became "vanity and vexation of spirit."[18]

Why did Solomon regress so far? He couldn't handle his promotion. Over the long haul, the fiber of his life began to break down. And then, staring at the sunlight of God's limitless blessings, he became blinded to his rightful role and calling.

Promotions Affect People

Finally, Nehemiah's advancement touched the lives of others. This is always true. You have no leader if you have no people. *Leading is a people-oriented job.* Nehemiah 5:18b says,

> Yet for all of this [all the abundance of food] I did not demand the governor's food allowance, because the servitude was heavy on this people.

I'm glad Nehemiah added these words because they provide a good balance to the matter of accomplishing projects.

Frequently, a strong leader will run roughshod over everybody else to achieve his objective. Nehemiah had a compassionate heart. He stayed sensitive to the needs of his people. It doesn't mean he lost control of his emotions and faltered in leadership. It means that Nehemiah, seeing that the people were overburdened and overtaxed, backed off and said, "Let's go at a reasonable pace. Let's keep in step with one another, tackling one problem at a time."

One leader put it like this:

> The man who is impatient with weakness will be defective in his leadership. The evidence of our strength lies not in streaking ahead but in a willingness to adapt our stride to the slower pace of our weaker brethren, while not forfeiting our lead. If we run too far ahead, we lose our power to influence.[19]

That's good advice for a strong leader. Nehemiah never lost his sensitive spirit.

Nowhere is Nehemiah's heart revealed more beautifully than in the midst of this passage that related to promotion. I have overlooked on purpose two phrases. First of all, notice part of verse 15: "I did not do so because of the fear of God."

Why didn't Nehemiah follow the former policies? His relationship to the Lord was so unshakable that when temptation came Nehemiah said, "How could I do that? My walk with God would be affected. I don't care what my salary is, what my privileges are, how deeply rooted the policies, or how great the position may be—*I can't do it.* My accountability to my Lord is the guiding point of my life. I fear Him too much to indulge myself."

Does that mean that people rightly related to God can't have nice things? Certainly not! But it does mean we are to guard against nice things having us. Let's hold onto everything loosely so that God can remove from our grasp whatever He'd like.

The second phrase that reveals Nehemiah's heart is in verse 19: "Remember me, O my God, for good, according to all that I have done for this people."

"Lord, I come before You," Nehemiah said, "and I say to You that I have been promoted by Your grace. I have accepted a position of great leadership. With the psalmist, I ask you to "Search me, O God, and know my heart: try me, and know my thoughts: And see if there be any wicked way in me" [Ps. 139:23–24, KJV]. And, Lord, if You find any problems with my soul, remove them and keep me in the center of Your will."

Being demoted is tough, but enduring a promotion is even tougher! Adversity forces us to trust, to wait on God, to lean on His arms for strength. But advancement can bring a host of difficulties: a false sense of pride, the temptation to take advantage of privileges, a battle with former policies, the tendency to miss the mark (the basic objectives), and an inclination to walk over people who are under our authority.

Small wonder Carlyle suggested only one in a hundred could pass the test of prosperity!

Nehemiah did. Do you?

9

Operation Intimidation

In typical fashion, when George Allen moved to Washington, D.C., as head coach of the Redskins, he promised the nation's capital the moon. He told them it would be just a few seasons before he would develop the Redskins into a championship football team. He promised them the Super Bowl by the second season.

The team had a brilliant preseason that first year. Then, early in the regular season, they won several amazing victories. It appeared the Redskins were to be lifted from their common role of loser to the uncommon role of winner. As time passed, however, the inevitable occurred. They began to lose and lose and lose. The blame fell, at least in part, not on Coach George Allen, but on a quarterback named Sonny Jurgenson, in my opinion one of the most gifted and effective quarterbacks to ever play the game. Jurgenson possesses a quality I deeply admire: personal security. It seems as though no one can intimidate Sonny Jurgenson.

One day after another defeat, Sonny was getting ready to take a shower and go home. A sports writer leaned over to him in the locker room and said, "Say, Sonny, be honest now. Don't all these off-the-wall remarks we write and all this public flak disturb you? Doesn't it make you want to quit when people throw things at you from the stands and when you get those dirty letters?"

Sonny just leaned back, gave a big, toothless grin, and sighed, "No, not really. I don't want to quit. I've been in this game long enough to know that every quarterback, every week of the season, spends his time either in the penthouse or in the outhouse."

Sonny's comment points out an important fact. It is true that if you are a leader, you spend your time either on the top or on the bottom. You seldom know what it's like to be in between. You are either the hero or the villain. You are respected or you are virtually hated. People in leadership must live on the yo-yo of public opinion, under the gun of verbal jabs as well as on the crest of great admiration. Being "in the outhouse" is a lot more difficult than those choice times "in the penthouse." It's when we are under verbal attack of the intimidating public that we show our colors.

I have discovered, after a number of years in the ministry, that this is true even in the spiritual realm. You commit yourself to a life of faith, you declare before God and man that you are going to walk with Him regardless, and suddenly, it happens! The enemy turns every gun he can upon you to blast you out of the saddle, to make you finish your season in defeat, to have you think that it's really not worth it after all.

A Well-timed Attack

Nehemiah, as reported in chapter 6, was not in the penthouse. Even though he had been a faithful, stable, and consistent leader, a plot to defeat him was underway. The attack upon Nehemiah was very significant because it happened at a crucial juncture in his life. It hit when he was nearly finished with the greatest task that Jerusalem's citizens had seen in their generation. Verse 1 tells us the attack occurred when they had almost finished rebuilding the wall. Not very long before they were ready to cut the ribbon and have a jubilant celebration, the enemy attacked.

That is so true to life that I can hardly believe it! This must be one of the reasons God says to the proud person to "take heed lest he fall" (1 Cor. 10:12). So often it isn't the person who has almost fallen who is vulnerable. It's the person who thinks he will *never* fall.

In Scripture, such failures happened time and again. When did Bathsheba cross the gaze of David? At a time when he had not known defeat in battle. From the time he took the kingdom until he fell with Bathsheba, David had not known defeat—politically, militarily, or personally. When did Jonah fall into self-pity? After the greatest revival that had ever swept over a city. When did Joseph receive that temptation from Mrs. Potiphar? Soon after he had been promoted under Mr. Potiphar's leadership and had been granted free run of the house.

Frankly, some of my most discouraging times occur on Mondays. I can't explain why. After a great Sunday, when we've been uplifted in one service after another, when we've heard testimonies and words of encouragement, when we've sung, had fellowship, worshiped and really enjoyed the Lord together, I sink into discouragement come Monday. I've also found when I am approaching a tremendous, mountaintop experience, I tend to slump into a low tide. Maybe you too have found this to be true.

A Subtle Strategy

Nehemiah was already planning the dedication service for the completed wall when the enemy attacked. Verse 2, through the end of the sixth chapter, tells us the story of these subtle attacks. There were three different kinds, each prompted by the enemy's same motive, which was to stop the project by deterring Nehemiah and his men through discouragement.

God permitted these tests to strengthen His servant. It is never the Lord's desire to soften us with ease and irresponsible luxury. That's unrealistic. That's penthouse living. Every once in awhile we are allowed to enjoy that kind of living, but not normally. G. K. Chesterton, Britain's nineteenth-century C. S. Lewis, put it this way: "Christianity has not been tried and found wanting; it's been found difficult and not tried."

Many a person today sees the demand of the Christian life and says, "You can have it. I would rather go my own way."

Nehemiah said, "I'm going God's way." Then came the attack. First of all, there was *a personal request*, which on the surface appeared to be quite innocent and harmless. In fact, it sounded like something he ought to do. Verse 2 says, "Sanballat and Geshem sent a message to me, saying, 'Come, let us meet together at Chephirim in the plain of Ono.'"

Now, the word *together* suggests the idea of a compatible visit. The plain of Ono was located about twenty miles north of Jerusalem, and it was a beautiful, verdant valley. Sanballat and Geshem were saying, "You need to get away for a while. You've been laying bricks too long, Nehemiah. We've had our spats, a few little disagreements, but let's get together. Come on up to Ono."

Nehemiah said, "Oh, no!" to Ono. "I'm not coming up there. Not on your life." Why Nehemiah's negative response? "They were planning to harm me" (v. 2). How did he know? I can't explain how any leader in God's marvelous family is gifted with a sixth sense from above. He gets to the edge of danger and something inside says, "I don't dare get into that; there's something wrong."

That doesn't mean we should live the life of an isolationist; it does mean we should live a life of discernment. Discernment is a God-given quality a leader must possess. Discernment allows you to read between the lines.

In this invitation, Nehemiah sensed trouble. He probably said to himself, "If I get up there in that place, I might be kidnapped. I could be murdered. I know for sure that as soon as I leave, the work here will suffer." So what did he do?

> But they were planning to harm me. So I sent messengers to them, saying, "I am doing a great work and I cannot come down. Why should the work stop while I leave it and come down to you?" (vv. 2b, 3).

To put it another way, there's a great difference between being an available man or woman of God and being a puppet of people. A *great* difference. Some people never understand how you can say no. But every leader under God must reserve that right. One of the marks of maturity is the ability to say no without explanation. But look at verse 4: "And they sent messages to me four times."

The messages kept coming! They probably were nice little embossed invitations with lovely printing; and each one had a note at the bottom: Request No. 2, Request No. 3, Final Request.

But each time Nehemiah gave the same answer: "I answered them in the same way" (v. 4). What a secure man! *Unintimidated* is the word. But he was about to face another pressure tactic in verse 5: "Then Sanballat sent his servant to me in the same manner a fifth time with an open letter in his hand."

First, there had been the personal requests. Now, here was an open letter. What did this mean? It was something like a petition. No longer was it a private letter in a personal envelope; this time the messenger came and opened it for everyone to read. Notice the intimidating, threatening remarks of this open letter (vv. 6, 7):

> "It is reported among the nations, and Gashmu says, that you and the Jews are planning to rebel; therefore you are rebuilding the wall. And you are to be their king, according to these reports. And you have also appointed prophets to proclaim in Jerusalem concerning you, 'A king is in Judah!' And now it will be reported to the king according to these reports. [Notice the intimidation.] So come now, let us take counsel together."

Allow me to elaborate on their tactics, reading between the lines: "You wouldn't come when we sent our invitation, and so we're letting the truth be known. We plan to expose you. We want everybody to know two things. First, when you came to Jerusalem, you had an evil motive. It was not just to rebuild the wall. You came for the express purpose of collecting a group of people around you so you could lead a revolution. Furthermore, your method is evil. You want to be the king and so you're spreading the prophets throughout the land to proclaim that Nehemiah will be the king, not Artaxerxes. So we're going to send the word back to the king in Persia. *Then* you'll come up and visit with us."

The Rumor Mill

What we're dealing with here is *rumor*. One of the characteristics of a rumor is that the source is never quoted. Actually, a source is seldom known. Verse 6 states, "It is reported among the nations. . . ." Who's the source of this "reporting"? Verse 6 also reveals the false conclusion that Nehemiah is going to be the king, "according to these reports."

A rumor is noted, first of all, because *the source is never declared.*

Second, a rumor is noted for its *exaggeration* and *inaccuracy*. A rumor spreads in an exaggerated fashion, and gullible listeners and gossips feed on that kind of garbage. They pass it from one mouth to the next ear, and by the time it comes to you, it is grossly inaccurate.

Have you ever played the party game "Gossip"? The first guy in a long line of ten people whispers something to the gal standing next to him. She whispers it quickly to the next one, and on it goes down the line. By the time it gets to person number ten, the message is garbled beyond belief. And that's with only ten people who are trying to cooperate!

A rumor leads to personal hurt and misunderstanding. What was the result of this report concerning Nehemiah? It hurt him—in fact it was *designed to hurt*.

Nehemiah was impaled on the horns of a dilemma. If he refused to go to Ono, it would be tantamount to saying, "I'm afraid to let the truth be known." But if he went to Ono, he would leave the work on the wall and would play into the hands of the enemy. He'd be in great danger. He was caught in what appeared to be an impossible situation.

I am personally convinced that the number one enemy of Christian unity is the tongue. It's not drink, not drugs, not poor homes, not inflation, not TV, not even a bad church program—it's the tongue.

People who spread rumors invariably display a lack of wisdom. Wisdom forces a person to ask such searching questions as, "Is it necessary to say this? Is this confidential information? Do I have any right to pass this on?" Wisdom prompts the reply, "Don't open your mouth because God hates those who sow discord among His family." (Of the seven things God hates, three relate to the tongue. See Proverbs 6:16–19.)

Another thing lacking from the rumormonger's act is *accurate information*. Anytime you want to find the truth, you have to first find the source. The proof of accuracy is, "Is this true? Can the original source be quoted?"

Further, rumor-spreaders lose sight of *the proper setting* for sharing information. A person needs to ask: "Will this benefit the person who hears me?" Or better than that, "Can he do anything about it? Or is this just going to be another pouring of useless hearsay into someone's ears?" When you give unverified information to people who are critical and negative, knowing they can't do anything about the situation anyway, that's an unwise move. When you go to an individual who can do something about relevant information and in a spirit of love share it, that is constructive criticism.

Now, not every critic is an enemy of the faith, nor is every person who criticizes of the devil. However, I'm not fully convinced that the term "critic" applies to the gossip. A person who is genuinely interested in the truth uses his tongue to secure and to maintain the truth.

What should be your response when you are confronted by a gossip? Frankly, I feel direct confrontation is the best response. The next time someone brings gossip or rumors to your ears, rebuke him. Chances are, you'll help teach a needed lesson.

In the case of Nehemiah, nobody was around as a witness to the truth. He was simply confronted with a letter of exposé that was built on a lie. Nehemiah responded beautifully. If you ever are the target of gossip, look carefully at verse 8. Here, you can learn how to handle yourself when you're under attack. For openers, Nehemiah calmly denied the charge: "Such things as you are saying have not been done." "It's not true," Nehemiah said. Then, he put the blame where it belonged: "But you are inventing them in your own mind."

"These are the things you have come up with in your head, and they are wrong," said Nehemiah. And verse 9 tells us he took his hurt to God. Nehemiah said,

> For all of them were trying to frighten us, thinking, "They will become discouraged with the work and it will not be done." But now, O God, strengthen my hands.

It is impossible for a leader—or any person for that matter—with a sensitive spirit not to be hurt by a rumor. I don't care how strong a leader you are, you will experience times when the cutting remarks really hurt. Afterwards, when you've picked up the pieces and put things back together, you'll be able to move on.

Let me say something to those who gossip. If your tongue is a loose tongue, God is going to have to deal with it. You see, gossip is a major reason for disunity in the family of God. The body has no stronger muscle than the one in our mouths!

What should we do then when we have disagreements that need to be expressed? We need to take them to the leaders who can do something about them, to those who will really listen, evaluate, and respond to what we have to say.

If you work in a corporation and are bad-mouthing your boss, you're wrong. You need to express that gripe to someone in authority in a tone that is loving and not harsh.

I believe every telephone ought to have written beside it the words of Ephesians 4:29:

> Let no foul speech whatever come out of your mouth, but only what serves well to improve the occasion, so as to add blessing to the listeners [MLB].[20]

This verse even covers proper criticism to the right person. Our words are supposed to edify, to build up.

Observe that the purpose of the letter to Nehemiah was to frighten him: "For all of them were trying to frighten us" (v. 9).

But Nehemiah didn't give in. He persisted in what he knew to be the will of God.

Isn't it interesting that when one approach didn't work, another approach was used. Enemies can be relentless! First, they tried to stop the project by a personal request. Second, they used the open-letter approach to halt progress. Finally, they employed a religious-sounding (yet intimidating) warning: "Run for your life!"

> And when I entered the house of Shemaiah the son of Delaiah, son of Mehetabel, who was confined at home, he said, "Let us meet together in the house of God, within the temple, and let us close the doors of the temple, for they are coming to kill you, and they are coming to kill you at night" (v. 10).

That's a frightening thing. Can you imagine what it was like? Some night Nehemiah put on his pajamas, blew out the candle, and after he laid down, he heard a noise outside. "Oh, no!" he said to himself. "That's one of those guys coming to get me!"

So this new memo said, "You know, Nehemiah, these guys are coming in the middle of the night, and they are going to get you. I'll tell you what, let's meet at the temple and we'll have a prayer together." You know, the super-pious approach—"Let's pray about this together." How phony can you get?

Nehemiah's discernment was remarkable. In verses 11 and 12 of chapter 6 he pondered: "Should a man like me flee? And could one such as I go into the temple to save his life? I will not go in."

That was so wise, but how did he know that? Again, I cannot explain it; verse 12 simply says, "Then I perceived that surely God had not sent him, but he uttered his prophecy against me because Tobiah and Sanballat had hired him."

Wow! Here's this strong leader, committed to building the walls, and a group of people have hired this "hit man" to corner him in the temple and finish him off. Nehemiah said, "I can't do that."

The dictionary says intimidation means "to compel or deter by a threat." To frighten by a threat. Do this—or else!

I have a pastor friend who once had a very successful ministry on the East Coast. The very first Sunday morning when he began this ministry, he found an unsigned letter on his desk. (They're usually unsigned.) The neat, well-printed letter said: "If you do not send your children to [such and such] Christian School, you will split the church." The note closed with the words "A concerned member."

That's intimidation. It's any attempt to get one's way by means of threat.

"Nehemiah, they're going to come in the middle of the night and they are going to get you. And if you don't get away, you've had it!" And Nehemiah replied, "I can't go."

"Why not?"

"Because God doesn't want me to go."

"Well, you're a fool."

"No. I'm walking by faith. I believe God will protect me."

Remember. God had said, "Nehemiah, don't go." Verse 13

says, "He was hired for this reason, that I might become frightened and act accordingly and sin."

Where was the sin? In yielding to an intimidating remark. It's not *being* intimidated, but *yielding* to intimidation that produces sin. Nehemiah said, "Before God, I can't give in." But why did his enemies want Nehemiah to sin? Verse 13 continues, "so that they might have an evil report in order that they could reproach me."

Soon nosy gossips would have been heard whispering to one another, "Did you hear about whom Nehemiah is spending time with these days? Every evening they're up at the temple together."

Nehemiah had just cause for his suspicion that rumors could very easily fly if he chose to accept this clandestine meeting at the temple. He was surrounded by people who kept that ancient postal service quite busy! "Also in those days many letters went from the nobles of Judah to Tobiah, and Tobiah's letters came to them" (v. 17).

Now this was *very practical*. Tobiah was his arch enemy—an unbeliever. He hated the things of God. Inside the wall was Nehemiah and a band of diligent men. But the plot was thickened because Tobiah, the enemy, was related by marriage and by blood to people on the inside; there was a constant passing of letters back and forth (in front of Nehemiah) about Nehemiah. Nehemiah reported that they kept sending these letters to one another.

> Moreover, they were speaking about his [Tobiah's] good deeds in my presence and reported my works to him. Then Tobiah sent letters to frighten me (v. 19).

Nehemiah said, "I'm not giving in. You can make all the trips to the temple at night that you want to, but I'm not going with you. Neither you nor a hundred like you will stop progress!"

Mission Accomplished!

Now look at verse 15. See what happens? What a magnificent accomplishment! "So the wall was completed. . . ." The final bricks were laid in the midst of one attack after another. Nehemiah was on the field under the gun; yet that wall went up. Verse 16 says:

And it came about when all our enemies heard of it [the completion of the wall], and all the nations surrounding us saw it, they lost their confidence.

That has to be the most thrilling experience in the world—to watch God come to the rescue when you have been helpless. In the middle of the incessant assault of the enemy, in spite of the endless verbal barrage, the wall was built! While the enemy blasts, God builds.

Why is this so important today? Because it is impossible to do the will of God, to walk by faith, to pass those bricks without attack. I encourage all who read these pages to stand firm. Remember John's counsel: "Greater is He who is in you than he who is in the world" (1 John 4:4).

The Lord strengthened Nehemiah through three severe attacks: (1) several personal letters, (2) an open letter impugning his motives and character, (3) a warning designed to paralyze him with fear. None of them worked! The wall continued to go up. Because Nehemiah and his workers were in the center of God's will, they were invincible. Persistence pays rich dividends.

I am reminded of those emphatic words Winston Churchill once delivered to the Harrow School: "Never give in! Never, never, never, never. Never give in!"

If honor is at stake, if a good principle is at stake, if you know you're in His will, never, *never* give in.

10
Revival At
Water Gate?

In every genuine revival in history, two major
thrusts have always appeared. First, there has always
been proclamation of the Bible, *God's Word;* second,
there has always been the responsive mobilization of the believers,
God's people.

Strange as it may sound, a revival does not relate directly to the
unsaved. You cannot revive the lost. You can revive the saved.
Revival occurs as God ignites the fire of His Word and mobilizes
His people to go and win the lost. Let me illustrate this concept of
revival from the pages of history.

Four hundred years ago in Germany, God lit a fire in the lives of
several men. As God burned His Word into the hearts of these few,
it wasn't long before such greater lights as Melanchthon, Calvin,
Zwingli, and, of course, Luther began to carry the torch to all of
Europe. The Bible came into the language and hands of the people
of Germany, and gradually the old formalism of the church was
replaced with living, vibrant Christianity. A lover of ancient liter-
ature has discovered an old Bohemian Psalter that has a picture of
Wycliffe striking the spark, Huss kindling the coals, and Luther
brandishing the flame. It says in effect, "Reformation has come!
Revival has occurred!" That Psalter is dated 1572. Even then they
realized what God was doing.

Not too many years later in Scotland there lived a fiery preacher
and a pungent writer named John Knox. He once said of Mary,

Queen of Scots, "She is an old Jezebel." When she heard of his remark, Mary responded, "I fear his tongue and pen more than the armies of England." She knew that Knox carried clout in the minds of the people. He read God's Word, trusted in its promises, and then mobilized the people of Scotland into what came to be known as the "Scottish Revival."

Then came the Wesley brothers. They lived in England in the 1800s. Born in a unique home, they were sons of an English rector and perhaps the greatest mother that England has ever known. In his fifty years of preaching, John delivered forty thousand sermons. He spoke to audiences as great as twenty thousand people without the assistance of a public address system. He traveled 225,000 miles, most of it on horseback, proclaiming the Word of God. His gifted brother Charles left the church a magnificent legacy of eight thousand hymns. Among them were many we still love to sing: "And Can It Be That I Should Gain?"; "O For A Thousand Tongues"; "Hark! the Herald Angels Sing"; "Christ for the World, We Sing"; "Arise, My Soul, Arise"; "Jesus, Lover of My Soul"; and on and on. The common people not only got a Bible, they got a hymnal. These were the two contributions Luther wished to make to Christendom: a Bible they could understand and a hymnal from which they could sing. He said, "Let them loose. The flame will spread on its own." That is revival. When the Word of God is proclaimed and the people of God are mobilized, revival has occurred.

The First Revival

Tucked away in the old Book of Nehemiah is the first recorded revival. And of all places, the revival occurred at Water Gate. According to Nehemiah 8:1, "And all the people gathered." In the setting of the first two verses of this chapter, the most exciting experience transpires since the wall was completed.

It is helpful to know that at this time there was a spiritual vacuum in the city. The wall reconstruction project had been completed and the people had moved into their own dwellings. According to chapter 7, which is a detailed chapter on organizational structure, the people were now well-ordered, well-defended, and well-governed. But in this community, even though its residents had nice homes and good jobs and were well-protected, there was still something missing. Nehemiah sensed the spiritual vacuum as did the people. A timeless truth emerges from all of this: It is not enough to have a well-constructed superstructure if there is little or no life on the inside. How true this is in the church! We've all seen beautiful structures and well-oiled organizational machinery, but later found that that was it.

Many a church is like an impressive machine I once read about. It had hundreds of wheels, cogs, gears, pulleys, belts, and lights, which all moved or lit up at the touch of a button. When someone asked, "What does it do?" the inventor replied, "Oh, it doesn't do anything—but doesn't it run beautifully?"

Machinery alone is not enough. This axiom also applies to the business world. Several significant industries are paying much attention to "clusters" and "groups" for employees, hoping to heighten their interest and involvement in each other and, of course, in the company.

Leaders, take note! Satisfactory buildings and a well-organized operation are essential. But getting your people grouped, protected, and relating smoothly with one another is equally vital. Those "walls" surely must be built, but a true and effective leader makes sure that what happens on the inside of the walls is for real too.

Three things happened in Nehemiah's day to ensure that the walls were put to proper use.

1. Fresh Personnel

Evidently, both the Lord and Nehemiah knew that Ezra would do a better job at getting things going inside that wall than would Nehemiah. Here is another example of entrusting the ongoing tasks of a project to others who are more adept and better qualified than the person at the top. We have already seen how Nehemiah was good at delegating tasks. Peter Drucker, the "final voice" on management in our day, would have been proud of him. He writes:

By now managers everywhere have learned that decentralization strengthens top management. It makes it more effective and more capable of doing its own tasks.[21]

Knowing this to be true, Nehemiah utilized the skills of Ezra at this crucial time in Jerusalem. Ezra became the spokesman before the people.

2. Established Truth

The Scripture was openly and boldly proclaimed. Often when success comes—be it in business or in the church—there is a tendency to operate on emotional fuel (enthusiasm, good feelings) instead of using the "authentic fuel" of established truth.

Remember that the first major thrust in a genuine revival is the proclamation of Scripture. The apostles, who set the pace for the early church, stayed with God's Word. Even when growth occurred and vast numbers of people became followers of Christ, those who led this first-century revival never ventured from the written Word of God. The same was true of the Reformers.

I find it helpful to discover in this section of Nehemiah's memoirs the characteristics of authentic Bible exposition. Beginning with the opening words of chapter 8, we read how the events transpired:

> And all the people gathered as one man at the square which was in front of the Water Gate, and they asked Ezra the scribe to bring the book of the law of Moses which the Lord has given to Israel. Then Ezra the priest brought the law before the assembly of men, women, and all who could listen with understanding, on the first day of the seventh month. And he read from it before the square which was in front of the Water Gate from early morning until midday, in the presence of men and women, those who could understand; and all the people were attentive to the book of the law (vv. 1–3).

First, there was the reading of God's Word. Exposition begins here—not with the opinion of man, but with the established truth of God.

Second, there was an obvious respect for the truth. People listened attentively.

> And Ezra opened the book in the sight of all the people for he was standing above all the people, and when he opened it, all the people stood up. Then Ezra blessed the Lord the great God. And all the people answered, "Amen, Amen!" while lifting up their hands; then they bowed low and worshiped the Lord with their faces to the ground (vv. 5,6).

Third, the truth was explained so that all who heard understood.

> And they read from the book, from the law of God, translating to give the sense so that they understood the reading (v. 8).

After an oral reading from the book, those gifted in its truths translated to give the sense or the meaning. The word *translated* means in Hebrew "to make something distinct," "to separate it from something else so as to make it flow together in a meaningful fashion." They separated the Word, the verses, the passages so that they fit into place in an intelligent, clear, and understandable fashion.

But why did they need to translate the Scripture? Remember, these people were Jews by birth but not by tongue or culture. These Jews, who had come from Babylon to Jerusalem, had brought with them a Chaldean mentality and lifestyle.

The words read to them were from the Hebrew Bible. They heard a Hebrew Bible through Babylonian ears. There was a communication breakdown. And so these trained scribes took the Hebrew text and made it meaningful to the ears of the listeners. After they had translated it, the verse says "they gave the sense." They unlocked the door leading to understanding—the ability to see something beneath the surface. They gave their audience an in-depth meaning of the words and passages so that understanding would result.

Fourth, the truth was applied. Those who heard it responded.

Then Nehemiah, who was the governor [that's something—the governor was right in the middle of the revival], and Ezra the priest and scribe, and the Levites who taught the people said to all the people, "This day is holy to the Lord your God; do not mourn or weep." For all the people were weeping when they heard the words of the law (v. 9).

Why were they crying? They knew they were guilty. They were thinking back to those years they had lived with no spiritual input. They also recalled the sins of their forefathers that had caused them to fall into captivity. The depth of their guilt brought weeping. (And that's a good sign, by the way. At times, guilt is an excellent motivational factor. Not all guilt is wrong. Guilt is often what God uses to bring people to a saving knowledge of Jesus Christ.)

In this moment of guilt, Nehemiah stood and said, "Now, stop that. God is forgiving. Let's move on. This is a holy day. This is a day not to cry but to celebrate." In verse 10 the multitude is told to:

"Go, eat of the fat, drink of the sweet, and send portions to him who has nothing prepared; for this day is holy to our Lord. [Don't cry on a holiday; celebrate on a holiday.] Do not be grieved, for the joy of the Lord is your strength."

Verse 11 says, "So the Levites calmed all the people, saying, "Be still, for the day is holy, do not be grieved."

It seems they were living in an era something like our 1960s during which some declared that God was dead. To the Jews of Nehemiah's time, God had been away on a long, weary journey; they had "lost touch" and were fearful of Him.

Recently I saw on the back of a camper a big black and white sign that said, "God is back, and boy is He mad." There's only one problem with that idea; God never left! Man's the one who left.

Those Jerusalem Jews were thinking, "God's been gone, but now He's back and He's mad." Nehemiah and his men were saying, "Oh, no. You are the ones who left! You should celebrate today. This marvelous God of heaven still stands with open arms and says, 'I'm ready to forgive and forget. I'll take everyone who will repent; come to Me just as you are. I'll take you.'"

Verse 12 tells us that they applied the message personally; they became a mobilized people:

> And all the people went away to eat, to drink, to send portions and to celebrate a great festival, because they understood the words which had been made known to them.

This was a revival! The Bible had been proclaimed and the people were mobilized.

As a wise leader, Nehemiah employed fresh personnel. As a godly leader, he stayed with the established truth. But there was yet another factor that gave meaning to the building of the wall.

3. Distinguishing Between the Means and the End

It's the old long-term, short-term distinction.

Nehemiah had been chosen to do essentially a short-term job, a means-to-the-end project rather than a comprehensive, end job. His leadership was to prevail over the building of the protective wall—a vital task but definitely not the *end* assignment. The purpose of the wall was not just to have a wall, but to contain, to protect, and to identify the people of God. Beyond the wall-building project was a goal Nehemiah never forgot.

Discerning leaders know how to distinguish the means from the end. Because they are free from tunnel vision, discerning leaders keep in mind the whole scene, not just their own contribution. Nehemiah made provision for the final completion of God's full plan. He wisely avoided the "monument mentality." He entertained no inflated opinions of the brick-and-mortar project. To him the wall afforded the people a useful and helpful environment (the means) for experiences in revival that would have eternal dimensions (the end).

If you think about the characteristics of Nehemiah's leadership revealed in this chapter, you will find a single theme threaded throughout: *unselfishness*. Unconcerned about having his name in lights, Nehemiah stepped aside and strengthened the overall project with fresh reinforcements—people like Ezra who was better than he in the handling of the Scripture. And as Ezra did his job, Nehemiah stood among the people applying the truth that was proclaimed. It posed no problem for him to step aside and have his wall project virtually ignored because a far more significant activity was taking place among the people. Why? His mindset was unselfish.

We have all seen leaders who do not have a servant's heart. They are nauseating examples of excessive image building. One authority, speaking of this type of leader, declared rather forcefully:

> The leader may consciously enjoy a feeling of superiority and aloofness, showing itself in condescension, vanity, conceit, and self-pride. He may demand too much adulation and personal loyalty, and therefore try to surround himself with sycophants, "Yes-men" and "rubber stamps." He may want his own way too much and too often, and be too opinionated and obstinate about taking counsel with his colleagues and followers.[22]

From the very start Nehemiah refused all temptations to turn the wall project into an ego trip. He was satisfied being an Indian among other Indians—not a chief.

May his tribe increase.

11

The Fine Art
of Insight

Baseball fans are all familiar with the seventh-inning stretch, when you get a chance to stand up and shake out the kinks before you settle down for the final innings. This is precisely what I suggest we do at this point with the book of Nehemiah. In review, let's brush the dust from a few of the previous chapters before we settle down with the last few verses of chapter 8 and proceed with the remainder of Nehemiah's story. To help stretch our mental muscles and sweep away a few cranial cobwebs, I'll approach our brief review from a different perspective.

A Glance Back And Forth

Think of the Book of Nehemiah as being divided into two main sections. In the first six chapters, there is a *reconstruction* of a wall; in the last seven, there is a *reinstruction* of the people who built that wall. The first six chapters tell the story of a dominant character (Nehemiah) who was the builder and superintendent over the job and ultimately became governor over the people of Jerusalem. But in the last seven chapters, the leadership shifts to Ezra who was a priest and scribe. Remember, he was the one who led the beginnings of the revival.

But there is threaded throughout the book one central theme, *leadership*—how God uses one person to motivate and encourage others into new fields, new vistas, new actions for change. In the first six chapters, God uses Nehemiah to teach us sound principles of leadership; in the last seven, He uses Ezra.

In the first part of Nehemiah 8, you will recall that the revival of the Word of God had a telling effect upon the people. Those who heard the Word read by Ezra were thrilled with what they heard. In fact, verse 8 says that they who read from the book translated it so that they gave the sense of it, and the result was *understanding*. In other words, the people who had built the walls and were now secure behind those walls began to have input from God's Word. It motivated them.

Input Vs. Insight

For a full day the people of Jerusalem had gathered facts from the Scripture. Let's call it "surface input." They absorbed an understanding of the facts so that their reservoir of biblical knowledge was enlarged. They received *input* but not *insight*. That was to come later.

Look at verse 13 of chapter 8:

> Then on the second day the heads of fathers' households of all the people, the priests, and the Levites were gathered to Ezra the scribe that they might gain insight into the words of the law.

The leaders of homes (the fathers) and the religious leaders (priests and Levites) met with Ezra to gain insight from God's Word.

The word *insight* is translated from a Hebrew verb that means "to be prudent," that is, to be wise, to have foresight. It's the idea of being shrewd in the practical management of one's daily affairs. Discernment and keen awareness are involved.

Insight is an essential trait for leaders. A leader must be able to see the big picture, to project into the tomorrows of any undertaking, to visualize the outworking of a plan. No leader can stay riveted to today. He must see the results of his "now" ahead of time.

Please understand that a vast knowledge of Bible facts is no guarantee of insight. You can have truth taught to you systematically, verse by verse, year after year, and still not gain insight. It's tragic, but it's true.

Remember the twelve disciples who helped serve the fish and bread to over five thousand people? This story is the only miracle recorded in all four of the Gospels. Jesus performed the miracle so that His disciples might realize He was able and had power in every circumstance in life. As they watched the loaves and fish multiply in His hands, you'd think they would have learned an invaluable lesson. But they didn't.

Only a few hours later, Jesus had them take a boat (without Him) across the Sea of Galilee. A storm blew in and they really got scared. It was dark and the clouds were terribly threatening. Christ soon discovered that they had short memories. Panic set in as they quickly forgot the lesson of the day before. Mark 6:51,52 tells it all:

> And He got into the boat with them, and the wind stopped; and they were greatly astonished, for they had not gained any insight from the incident of the loaves, but their heart was hardened.

Hadn't they been exposed to Christ and His miracle? Yes. Hadn't they heard His teachings about being "the bread of life"? Absolutely. They had received *input* but not *insight*.

It's one thing to know the theory of a job and to have a head full of knowledge about proper management, directing people, and accomplishing objectives. But it's another thing entirely to conduct oneself with insight—to lead people insightfully.

For about five years I worked in a machine shop—first as an apprentice and finally as a journeyman machinist. One of my foremen was a man who knew the machinist trade like you know the palm of your hand. Seasoned for more than thirty years, his knowledge of the field was vast. But he had little insight. He lacked wisdom and foresight in dealing with the men who worked under him. This led to numerous conflicts and a large turnover of personnel in his department. No man in the shop knew more about the trade or less about leading others in the practical assignments of getting the job done.

Pursuing Insight

Since it is clear that insight is a valuable virtue for leaders to possess, let's think about how it is acquired.

In Nehemiah 8:13–15 there are three specifics about gaining insight. To begin with, *it takes time*. No one suddenly becomes wise. David declared in Psalm 119:100 that you don't have to be old to have understanding. But you and I should realize there is no such thing as instant insight. No novice in the Christian life has a depth of insight. You will notice in verse 13 that they came back to Ezra on the second day. That's a pretty good hint that you can't gain insight on the first encounter.

I discovered something else here. To pursue insight not only takes time, *it takes the right people*. Look again at verse 13. These men came to one individual, Ezra, that they might gain insight from him.

I often recall with great delight my days as a pastoral intern. It was between my second and third years at Dallas Theological Seminary. Ray Stedman, pastor of Peninsula Bible Church in Palo Alto, California, had invited my wife Cynthia and me to spend the summer of 1961 at the church. One of my goals was to gain a working knowledge of how a church functions. I also had been praying that God would allow me to rub shoulders with some wise and godly men. Without realizing it, I was seeking to gain insight as a young leader.

On several occasions I had the privilege of spending time with Dr. Dick Hillis, the former president of Overseas Crusades. Through time spent with him I gleaned "chunks" of insight. The same thing occurred as a result of lengthy times spent with Bob Smith, Ray Stedman's associate for many years. What rich memories these are! I can't recall any "facts" those two men taught me, but the insights I gained still influence my thinking. As the Scottish people say, "It was more felt than 'telt.'"

There's a third area to be discussed when we consider the pursuit of insight; *it takes the right attitude*. Verse 13 mentions the "heads of fathers' households of all the people, the priests, and the Levites" were gathered to hear Ezra. I'm sure some of them were older than he; some were grandfathers, others were scribes. These men were members of Ezra's peer group; yet they said, "Teach us." They really wanted to learn.

Some of the wealth of information that God has for us will come through our peers, but our attitude must be right.

As I discuss attitude, I'm reminded of a young couple with several small children who recently attended a family conference where I spoke. Though they looked and sounded like a Christian family, it was apparent that their lives were very miserable. I'm sure divorce was on the back burner of their minds. However, as the week progressed, I watched the couple change as they sat under the teaching of God's Word.

Another conference speaker, Olan Hendrix, spoke in the mornings on the making of the man of God, and his messages seemed to dovetail beautifully with my comments during the evening sessions on "Insights into Family Living" where I shared things pertaining to husband-wife, parent-child relationships.

As time passed, the father hung on every word. The mother had her Bible open and stayed right with us from passage to passage. On the last day of the family conference, the young couple came up to my wife and me and said, "We want you to know that this week has been a 180-degree turn-around experience for us. When we came, we were ready to separate. We're going back stronger than we have ever been in our marriage." Now that's the sort of thing that makes you want to stick your arms up and say, "Hallelujah!"—except for the fact that there is another story as heartbreaking as the first is heartwarming.

At the same conference with the same speakers, the same truths, the same surroundings, the same schedule, another father was turned off. He wasn't open. He attended the first few sessions, but by and by the guilt became so great and the conviction so deep that he went home. He had stayed awake the entire night before and reached the decision to leave and not come back. His family left hurting—perhaps even more than when they came. What was the difference? Attitude.

Some people come to meetings or church services and it does

nothing. In fact, it turns them off. Others cannot get enough. Just like sponges, they get bigger and bigger—*spiritually*. They get more of the Water of Life and grow larger and larger. I see them and think, "Man, there's no end to this. This is the most exciting thing I have ever seen!" What's the difference? It's the attitude. They have a teachable spirit. The soil has been prepared and their heart is open, saying, "Welcome, God. Speak to me." And when He speaks, what a remarkable change! But the person with an unteachable attitude, a closed heart, will never gain insight until the "internals" are changed. The longer I live, the more I value the importance of attitude.

Let's review before proceeding. To gain insight, leaders need *time*. Time to think, to meditate, to soak up the whole scene. Next, leaders need to be with the *right people*. Insight is often "rubbed off" from one life to another. Finally, insight comes as we maintain the right *attitude*—an open, teachable mind. These three qualities alone will help make you a unique leader.

The Results Of Insight

When we get beneath surface facts and start to traffic in the realm of in-depth truth, two things usually happen: (1) we walk in total obedience, and (2) we discover genuine happiness.

Those leaders in Nehemiah's day experienced both. Read the last five verses of chapter 8 for yourself. If you can mentally picture the scene, you'll end up smiling.

God told them to go live in booths. Those intelligent, grown men—all respected leaders—were to go out, fetch some branches and sticks, and make booths for their families to live in. Imagine that! But out of obedience, they built and lived in shacks as God had required.

Can't you see Sanballat and Tobiah standing outside the wall? Everybody is leaving, looking for sticks and branches.

The enemies ask, "Where are you going?"

"I've got to go get some sticks."

"You're going to go get some what?"

"We're going to go get some sticks."

"For what?"

"For shacks."

"You're going to go get some sticks for some shacks?"

"Right. Come on, kids. There are some branches over here and I want you to carry a handful back."

After a while, they get all their sticks and leaves bundled up and walk back into the city. Old Sanballat is still looking over the wall, taking it all in. Some guy up on his roof is putting together a little lean-to, and it's no beauty! These shacks looked like dumps, and they were all over the city of Jerusalem.

Sanballat must have shaken his head in amazement and mumbled, "Wow, they not only build lousy walls; they can't build houses either! Look at those miserable shacks." But regardless of how strange it appeared, the people obeyed.

When God gives you insight (not just knowledge), you say, "Lord, take over. Nothing in my life is private. Here are the keys." Total, unreserved obedience comes as a result of gaining insight.

Look at what it says in Nehemiah 8:17:

And the entire assembly [no holdouts!] of those who had re-turned from the captivity made booths and lived in them. The sons of Israel had indeed not done so from the days of Joshua the son of Nun to that day. . . .

They obeyed. Those men said, "God says build a booth; so we'll build a booth."

And amazing though it may sound, those people were happier than they had ever been. "And there was great rejoicing," wrote Nehemiah. I can't explain how it happens, but when you do what is right, you're happy. When you do what is wrong, you may make millions, but you're miserable. Isn't that remarkable? How could a family live happily in a little shack? They were happy because they were obedient. Since the dads in the home had gained insight as leaders, they had obeyed the Lord completely. And God gave them happiness.

Let's face it, your average, standard bosses are a dime a dozen. People in authority over others are found in abundance. In every sizable corporation, organization, or military unit, there are those who give orders and outrank the majority. But few of them are leaders with insight, that is, perspective, wisdom, or a depth of awareness. With that single quality at work in your leadership, you'll be a rare find!

Believe me, insightful leadership is attainable. Nehemiah had it. So did Ezra. But they had no "corner" on this virtue. No one does. It is available to all who are willing to pay the price.

Insight not only will give you a perspective on the past and enable you to face the future with confidence and vision, but it also will give you an honest appraisal of *yourself*, especially in the area of priorities. In fact, priorities are what my next chapter is all about.

12
Putting First
Things First

A California industrialist addressed a group of executives at a leadership seminar some time ago. His topic concerned employee motivation—how to get the job done while maintaining the enthusiasm and commitment of your personnel. He offered a lot of helpful advice, but one concept in particular has stuck in my head: "There are two things that are the most difficult to get people to do: to think . . . and to do things in the order of their importance."[23]

That concept touches the very nerve center of leadership. How difficult it is to find a person who really thinks first—and then acts! Most of us usually do the opposite. Equally difficult is the task of helping people to maintain proper priorities and to use their time wisely. Not only does the leader wrestle with ways to help others think and put first things first, he struggles to do this *himself*. However, the better he can maintain these two disciplines, the better he will lead.

I appreciate the story of Nehemiah very much because he was a man who thought before he acted and knew what his priorities were.

Taking Time to Think

As you recall, Nehemiah didn't bring a group of people into Jerusalem and immediately have them start to stack up bricks and erect a wall. He first spent four months in uninterrupted thought. He came to live with the vision before he ever shared it with anyone else. He pored over it in thought before God. Only then did he come into that city and begin to build a wall.

When opposition came, he didn't instantly retaliate; he thought it over instead. He planned out before God the best way to handle the interruption or the opposition, and then he acted wisely. When the time came to develop the plan for a righteous life-style, what we would call a good government, he didn't suddenly plunge into it; he first spent some more time *thinking*. And the people, apparently imitating the thoughtful approach exemplified by Nehemiah, also went to God in prayer. Their prayer, the longest recorded prayer in the Bible (Neh. 9:5–38), revealed their utter repentance and confidence in Jehovah. Over a lengthy period of thinking, planning, and reflecting, they came to a conclusion, which is recorded in the last verse of that long prayer. Before we look at that conclusion, let's think about thinking.

Thinking is hard work. Don't kid yourself—coming up with a good plan is usually far more difficult than carrying it out. Leaders who don't plan carefully and shoot from the hip miss the target— and they wound others while firing!

Wives want to have husbands who think through their philosophy on the home and the family. Few things are more frustrating than trying to please a man who hasn't declared what he wants. Here are some questions we men should think through:

- What are the goals of our home?
- What is the best way to inculcate our Christian convictions?
- Where shall we live? Why?
- How should we try to reach our neighbors and friends for Christ?
- Why do we want children?
- What can we do to help each child become confident and fulfilled?
- Which methods of discipline shall we use?
- What do we want to accomplish on our vacations?
- How involved should we be in the church? In civic affairs? In athletics?

- What are our convictions regarding music?
- How shall we cultivate a close relationship as husband and wife?
- What guidelines on teen-age dating will we follow?

Men, that kind of thinking is hard work! But what a difference it would make in your leadership in your home if you'd think through such issues.

Another set of questions could be drawn up regarding your leadership at work. Anything worth doing is worth taking the time to do right.

Thinking includes praying and quietness. We've seen Nehemiah often on his knees. He prayed through vital issues. So must we. We've also seen him quiet, silently thinking through his plans. How very important that was. Free from rush and panic, Nehemiah's deliberate plans gave others a definite sense of confidence. Frequent last-minute changes and shallow, off-the-cuff decisions irritate those who follow. They fear the consequences that could affect them.

Thinking calls for projecting. By backing off and thinking through a plan, the leader is able to travel down his projected path intelligently and to face future inevitabilities—while it is still safe.

Jesus spoke of the wisdom of thinking ahead and planning this way.

"For which one of you, when he wants to build a tower, does not first sit down and calculate the cost, to see if he has enough to complete it? Otherwise, when he has laid a foundation, and is not able to finish, all who observe it begin to ridicule him, saying, 'This man began to build and was not able to finish.' Or what king, when he sets out to meet another king in battle, will not first sit down and take counsel whether he is strong enough with ten thousand men to encounter the one coming against him with twenty thousand?" (Luke 14:28–31).

Leaders who expect to be respected and followed must first and foremost be *thinkers*.

Documenting the Priorities

As we consider the story of Nehemiah, we find the people anxious to alter their lives. In short, they determined to do things in the order of their importance. First things were to come first. The people were thoughtfully remembering the past and saying to the Lord, "Because of all these things we have brought before You, our Father, we want to establish some priorities. We are making an agreement in writing." These priorities are dealt with in Nehemiah 9. In this lengthy chapter, the people pour out their souls to God. They verbally declare their dependence. In effect, they develop a new set of priorities, which they document in writing.

The document:

> Now because of all this we are making an agreement in writing; and on the sealed document are the names of our leaders, our Levites and our priests (Neh. 9:38).

Do you see what they did? They were really serious about putting first things first. Signatures accompanied this "sealed document" (see Neh. 10:1–27) so that all would know they meant business. You see, coming to terms with priorities is extremely important. Unfortunately, many who read this will nod in agreement but will not follow through any further than that.

Nehemiah's peers prayed, "Lord, we don't want this to be simply an empty series of words. We want it to be a promise that is nailed down. We declare our dependence. We'll sign our names to prove that we'll keep our promise!"

Before we proceed to the promises they made in their document, let's discover something about those who signed the agreement. If you look at Nehemiah 10, you will discover a list of eighty-four names. Nehemiah's name is first. Following Nehemiah, you'll find the names of twenty-two priests (vv. 1–8); seventeen Levites (vv. 9–18); and forty-four others who were called leaders or heads of homes (vv. 10–27).

More important than mere names, though, is what verse 28 says was true of every name that appeared on the document:

Now the rest of the people, the priests, the Levites, the gate-keepers, the singers, the temple servants, and all those who had separated themselves from the peoples of the lands to the law of God, their wives, their sons and their daughters, all those who had knowledge and understanding.

We learn two things that characterized the people whose names appeared on the petition: (1) they had separated themselves from all the heathen and their lifestyle; and (2) they had an understanding of what they were doing. This tells us that no little children signed the agreement. They wouldn't have been able to understand. It also tells us that in order to sign the document, a person had to understand that the appearance of his name meant he would be distinctively unique and unlike the pagans surrounding him.

You should pay attention in particular to a portion of verse 28:

And all those who had separated themselves from the peoples of the lands to the law of God, *their wives, their sons and their daughters* (italics added).

This refers, I suppose, to the age group we would call "twenty and under." Although the names of some sons and daughters appeared on the document, not all the names were listed. Verse 28 begins "Now the rest of the people. . . ." There were others besides these who were willing to say, "We're going to be distinct individuals and not be concerned about conformity in matters that really pertain to life." I am suggesting that they were putting first things first *regardless* of the situation.

Why was it important for them to do this? Because they drove a "literary stake" into the ground that day. It became a rallying point; they erected a written monument that said in effect, "This is our promise to you, O God. This is our constitution, our declaration of distinction. We don't care if anyone else in the world lives by this. We will live by it. It will be our guide. Our homes will be distinct. Our philosophy of life will not be like that of those who live outside the walls—or even of some who live within the city's walls. This is something, Lord, that we want to carry out before You."

Before discussing the actual promises the people made, let's consider the matter of *documenting* our priorities.

As a minister I marry as many as forty couples a year. This means a lot of new homes are established. It would be easy for me to just stand with them, say a few religious clichés, pronounce them husband and wife, and walk away whistling "Here Comes the Bride." But I have determined not to do that.

Before I will marry any couple, I require at least three premarital counseling sessions with them. Among other things, I ask them to begin formulating their priorities as a couple. I ask them to write them down, to *document* their priorities, which later I read during their ceremony and occasionally weave into the wording of their vows. I then ask them to listen to a tape recording of their ceremony every year when their anniversary rolls around. Hopefully, this annual exercise will reinforce some specifics that will help each couple determine if they are still on target. The same procedure could be used in getting a college education, in establishing a business, or in undertaking any large project. Written priorities don't get vague or fuzzy.

The promises. In Nehemiah 10:29 there is a general promise *to obey* what God had declared. In verse 30, the people specifically said that they would obey Him in their *homes.*

That really makes sense. They were surrounded by heathen tribes and pagan people who marched to a different drumbeat. The easiest thing in the world would have been to lose their distinctiveness as "the people of God," and so the leaders of each home promised (v. 30): "We will not give our daughters to the peoples of the land or take their daughters for our sons."

They said, "We won't shrug our shoulders, yawn, and say, 'It doesn't matter' when our kids want to mix and mingle with the crowd." Distinctive, respectable leaders have distinctive, respectable homes.

The point I want to make very clear is this: When morals of a nation are under stress, the home is the first to suffer. Evangelist Billy Graham put it this way:

> The immutable law of sowing and reaping has held sway. We are
> now the hapless possessors of moral depravity and we seek in vain

for a cure. The tares of indulgence have overgrown the wheat of moral restraint. Our homes have suffered. . . . When the morals of society are upset, the family is the first to suffer. The home is the basic unit of society and a nation is only as strong as her homes.[24]

If you're thinking about documenting a list of priorities for living, I suggest you start with the home.

Next, the signers promised to *conduct business* in an obedient manner. Verse 31 says:

> As for the peoples of the land who bring wares or any grain on the sabbath day to sell, we will not buy from them on the sabbath or a holy day; and we will forgo the crops the seventh year and the exaction of every debt.

This promise was not meaningless. These were people who got hungry and maybe didn't have another good day for buying and selling. They would doubtless be tested by the peoples of another culture. But still they say, "When the Saturday Sabbath begins and we see those who want to do business coming over the hills toward Jerusalem, we will say, 'Not open. We'll talk with you tomorrow.' And when the seventh year rolls around, we'll rest from sowing and reaping until the next year. When our brother owes us a debt, we will look on it as God would have us look on it. There will be a release from the debt. Our business dealings will be on the up-and-up."

The distinction of a godly leader is that when he does business, he does it with integrity. When he puts in a day's work, he puts in a *day's* work. When he is to check in at a certain time, he is punctual. When he is trusted to not take what does not belong to him, he leaves it. When he completes his expense account, he does not pad the record.

Keith Miller puts it this way:

> It has never ceased to amaze me that we Christians have developed a kind of selective vision which allows us to be deeply and sincerely involved in worship and church activities and yet almost totally pagan in the day in, day out guts of our business lives and never realize it.[25]

In the nuts and bolts of living, God will honor the person who honors Him. Such a decision deserves a place on any leader's priority list.

The Jews had declared they would put first things first in their homes and in their business activities. Next they turned their attention to their *place of worship*. Nine times in Nehemiah 10:32–39 the "house of the Lord" or the "house of God" is mentioned. It's not difficult to catch the theme:

> We also placed ourselves under obligation to contribute yearly . . . for the showbread. . . . Likewise we cast lots for the supply of wood among the priests, the Levites, and the people . . . and in order that they might bring the first fruits of our ground and the first fruits of all the fruit of every tree . . . annually. . . . We will also bring the first of our dough [coarse meal], our contributions, the fruit of every tree (vv. 32–35,37).

Putting it all together, verse 39 concludes: ". . . we will not neglect the house of our God."

Now wait a minute! We have labeled the priority in this passage the *place of worship*. In Nehemiah's day it was the temple. God lived there. So when they came to the house of God, they brought with them all these things because it was the place of God's dwelling. But when Christ our Lord died, the veil was torn in two, it was split from top to bottom. Where does God live now? On earth He lives in every believer.

Once, when Augustine was tempted to plunge into the old life, he said, "Thou fool, dost not thou know that thou art carrying God around with thee." How right he was! The house of God is *right within you*. Talk about a mind-boggling concept! Talk about removing the old sacred secular divisions in life. I'm saying that the place of highest priority in these verses is the inner man where Jesus Christ resides, where the Holy Spirit has built His temple. Paul states it clearly:

> Or do you not know that your body is a temple of the Holy Spirit who is in you, whom you have from God, and that you are not your own? For you have been bought with a price: therefore glorify God in your body (1 Cor. 6:19,20).

Are you neglecting the temple? In the days of Nehemiah the temple was not a place where people just walked by and said, "Wow! God lives over there. Have you been over there lately?" It was the place where they worshiped with great care and a sensitive, delicate spirit. How are you treating God's house?

I have one other question: Is your temple clean? You're not trying to communicate distinctive leadership principles from a dirty container, are you? Habits that harm your health will hinder your impact and confuse those who look to you for direction.

Priorities are rather convicting, aren't they?

Key Principles to Remember

There are some very simple—but life-changing—principles that I glean from these verses in Nehemiah 10. The first is that *serious thought precedes any significant change.* You never change areas of your life that have not been given serious thought. We need to schedule some quiet times in our lives, times for thinking and reflection.

When you see a person who has changed from what he was a year ago and you ask him, "Hey, how did that come about?" he will never say, "Oh, it just happened. It's amazing; it surprised even me! I didn't plan for it to happen, I just changed." Instead, he will tell you, "I'm glad you asked," and he'll go on to describe what God did—one, two, three, four. Change comes on the heels of deep, honest thinking about our lives.

Second, *written plans confirm right priorities.* Do you really want to maintain the right priorities? Write them down! I suggest you begin to keep a journal. You may have some ideas floating around in your head, but they need to be nailed down. I learned years ago that thoughts disentangle themselves when spoken or put in ink. Your thoughts are good, but they are entangled because they haven't been thought through and written down. Your being able to put first things first will never happen until some vital things are written out, word for word.

Third, *a loss of distinction and conformity to the world go hand in hand.* Do you want to know today whether you have really conformed to this world or not? Check out your distinction. I don't mean you should check out your religious lifestyle. I mean, check on your authenticity compared to New Testament Christianity. Look at your life, your home, your work, your worship, and then ask yourself, "Am I really distinct? Could a person read the real me and see God's message on display?"

The leaders who have meant the most to me in my life are those who are authentic people. They are men and women who have thought before they acted, who have put first things first, and who have maintained their distinctiveness as Christian ladies and gentlemen. I thank God on every remembrance of them.

Think. Then do the things that need to be done in the order of their importance. People gravitate to leaders who live by that philosophy. I did, and I'll never be the same because of it.

13
The Willing Unknowns

The bicentennial celebration of our nation was an unforgettable experience. My wife and I were part of a tour in 1976 that traveled for two weeks along the East Coast, and we were thrilled by our visits to the immortal sights where America's cradle first rocked. Monuments and memorials, buildings and bridges, towns and tombs seemed to speak with eloquent voices from the past. The great statesmen became familiar names: George Washington, Thomas Jefferson, Benjamin Franklin, Patrick Henry. We are forever indebted to them for their capable leadership and patriotic zeal.

But there is another body of names and faces equally deserving of our praise. They are the lesser lights, the forgotten heroes, the unknowns, the "nobodies" who paved the way for the "somebodies." Without these willing unknowns, no leader can ever carry out his calling. But how easy it is to forget them.

This was brought home to me rather forcefully one day when my family and I were driving down the coast of California from San Francisco to Los Angeles. As we traveled along, enjoying the crashing surf to our right and the distant mountains to our left, we were laughing, singing, and having a great time. It was one of those delightful moments large families enjoy together.

It wasn't long, however, before things got quiet. As we went over the crest of a hill, we saw literally thousands of small white crosses standing at attention in perfect rank and file. Our youngest child leaned toward me and asked, "Daddy, what's all that?" Almost without thinking I answered, "Son, that's a military graveyard. That's a place where they have buried the men and women who died in battle. Few people remember them, Son, but they are the reason we are free today." His eyes got big as he gazed in silence across that hillside.

The car stayed very quiet. I slowed down and we stared as we passed by. I confess to you that I swallowed a big knot in my throat as there hung in my head the words of John McCrae. He was a poet who penned these thoughts expressing the viewpoint of the dead speaking to the living:

> In Flanders fields the poppies blow
> Between the crosses, row on row.
> That mark our place; and in the sky
> The larks, still bravely singing, fly.

As we drove on, I thought of how true that really is. The crosses stand in rows. The larks fly by. The cars speed on. Every once in a while the unknown dead must say, "Don't forget us. We are the reason you are able to drive and live and move freely in this great nation." There they lie, the willing unknowns.

Two dangers lurk in the shadows of leadership. One is the *reluctance* on the part of the leader to become virtually unknown, forgotten, and overlooked in the accomplishment of the objective. The second is the *negligence* of strong, natural leaders who fail to recognize others who really deserve much of the credit. It's the second danger I want to strongly emphasize in this chapter, but before doing so, let's take time to consider the first.

I'm going to ask you to make a commitment to the Lord to be, if necessary, utterly unknown in your position of influence. This is the way great, godly leaders are. If you desire fame and recognition, you will most likely fail as a leader and your efforts will go unrewarded for all eternity. That's not a threat: it's a promise.

Do you recall what Jesus taught?

> Beware of practicing your righteousness before men to be noticed by them; otherwise you have no reward with your Father who is in heaven (Matt. 6:1).

— 150 —

And in even stronger words, He declared:

> "You know that the rulers of the Gentiles lord it over them, and
> their great men exercise authority over them. It is not so among
> you, but whoever wishes to become great among you shall be your
> servant, and whoever wishes to be first among you shall be your
> slave; just as the Son of Man did not come to be served, but to
> serve, and to give His life a ransom for many" (Matt. 20:25–28).

All of us can name leaders who became almost obscure for the
sake of getting a job done. It sounds strange to our twentieth-
century ears, but God is ready to bless some unique leaders who
genuinely do not care who gets the glory. Such leaders are all too
rare, but it's beautiful to stumble across a few outstanding people
in life who don't have to be superstars; they willingly remain unknown and authentic servants.

Identifying The Unknowns

Now let's consider the other side of the coin: how to give credit
to the many unknowns who delight in filling support positions so
that the job will get done. Several people like this appear in the
eleventh chapter of Nehemiah's journal, a chapter we could entitle
the "Flanders' field" of the Bible. We find here the crosses of unknown (and unpronounceable!), obscure, forgotten people. But
they represent a massive force that makes the Word of God exciting. You cannot appreciate the names and people of Nehemiah 11,
however, if you do not know the reason they appear. Nehemiah
7:1–2 provides a little background information:

> Now it came about when the wall was rebuilt and I had set up the
> doors, and the gatekeepers and the singers and the Levites were
> appointed, that I put Hanani my brother, and Hananiah the com-
> mander of the fortress, in charge of Jerusalem, for he was a faithful
> man and feared God more than many.

The names of these two men are unfamiliar and nothing more is
said of them. But they were among the willing unknowns. They

were the delegates who carried out the wishes of Nehemiah, the governor.

Then verse 3 says that Nehemiah set up a schedule for the city:

> Do not let the gates of Jerusalem be opened until the sun is hot, and while they are standing guard, let them shut and bolt the doors. Also appoint guards from the inhabitants of Jerusalem, each at his post, and each in front of his own house.

So there was a security system. A police force had been established and was being maintained, and some form of normal living had begun. The city had everything except the most important ingredient—people.

Look at verse 4: "Now the city was large and spacious but the people in it were few and the houses were not built." Remember the little couplet you used to say when you were a little child as you folded your hands together?

> Here's the church, and here's the steeple;
> Open the door, and see all the people!

I suppose a similar couplet could have been hung over the main entrance to Jerusalem:

> Here's the wall, and here's the city;
> Open the gates; my, what a pity!

There were no people. Why build a wall around rubble? Because to the Jew, Zion was to be honored. It was the place of God's delicate handiwork in the lives of His chosen people.

Why weren't there many people in the city of Jerusalem? First of all, the city had been without a wall for 160 years. If my calculations are correct, the Jews spent seventy years in captivity, and an additional ninety years passed before Nehemiah came on the scene. So for more than 160 years, Jerusalem was little more than a pile of debris, a huge "dumping yard." If you lived there, you were open prey to all enemies. So what had the people done? They had built themselves spacious, lavishly furnished homes in the suburbs. Most of the Jews had forsaken an urban life.

The other reason for the lack of people was the fact that if you moved into the city, you had a lot of work ahead of you—debris, stones, and stumps were everywhere.

So, how would they get people into the city? That must have bothered the Jerusalem Chamber of Commerce of Nehemiah's day. They had to come up with a plan.

Look at verse 1 of Nehemiah 11. Did *anybody* live in Jerusalem? Yes, the members of the chamber of commerce did: "The leaders of the people lived in Jerusalem." They had to, you know; it was part of their job. That's the way they got an annual bonus—it probably was part of an incentive plan to encourage living in the city. But the rest of the people didn't. They lived outside in the surrounding, attractive hamlets of the valley—the suburbs.

Two things caused the people to move back into Jerusalem. First, *they cast lots* to bring one out of ten into the urban area. This group came by force. It was something like the way the U.S. Government drafted men into the military during the Vietnam War. When a man's number came up, he went.

But the second method of gaining population is of even greater interest to us. According to Nehemiah 11:2, *another group volunteered:* "And the people blessed all the men who volunteered to live in Jerusalem." Verse 1 did not mention volunteers. That verse said if the lot fell on you, you and your family were forced to move into the city. No choice was involved.

Among the nine-tenths who remained outside the wall, there were some who were strangely moved of God to give themselves to urban dwelling. What makes this significant is the word translated *volunteered.* It is a Hebrew word that means "to impel, to incite from within." Inherent in the word is the idea of inner generosity and willingness. In other words, down deep inside, these volunteers were stirred up; they were impelled by God to move. And they did.

Can you imagine it? These people, living in the suburbs, were pinpointed by God to move from suburbia into the inner city, and they did it willingly and generously. Had they never volunteered, the city would hardly have prospered, nor could it have withstood the enemy attacks that came in later years.

Devotion Of The Nameless

One scholar has done a rather intricate work of calculation and has determined that there were probably a million or more people living in areas surrounding Jerusalem. A tenth of those people moved by force, but a large number of them came inside the city because they were impelled from within. They became, to use my title, "the willing unknowns." The Scripture hardly mentions the name of a single one of them.

It is a fact that "willing unknowns" never have their names in lights. In the Book of Exodus, chapter 35, we find a group of people who were skilled craftsmen in embroidery, weaving, and other skills. They were the ones who added the finer touches to the tabernacle. Exodus 35 refers to those who willingly gave their substance, their talent, and their service for the things of God. The same Hebrew word for *volunteer* found in Nehemiah 7 also appears in Exodus 35. They volunteered themselves to God. Hardly a name is remembered except Moses, the leader, and Aaron, his illustrious brother. But the whole tabernacle beautification project would have failed without the willing unknowns.

Deeds Of The Nameless

In Nehemiah 11, I find five specific groups who willingly gave something—even though their giving remained anonymous.

We've just read about the first group: "The people blessed all the men who volunteered to live in Jerusalem" (v. 2).

Group 1 included *those who willingly moved into the city.* They pulled up their domestic roots, left their lovely homes, started over from scratch, submitted themselves to a government they hadn't elected, and lived in a city policed by a group of people they didn't know. Although they seemed to be insignificant, they were very important because they became the new inhabitants of the city.

We find the second group mentioned in Nehemiah 11:10–12:

> From the priests: Jedaiah the son of Joiarib, Jachin, Seraiah the son of Hilkiah, the son of Meshullam, the son of Zadok, the son of

Meraioth, the son of Ahitub, the leader of the house of God and their kinsmen who performed the work of the temple, 822.

There were 822 people *who willingly worked within the temple.* That's quite a staff! This group volunteered for work in the house of worship.

So now we have two "volunteer" groups: those who moved into the city, and those already in the city who gave themselves willingly to the ministry within the temple. This second group faithfully supported the work with their talents and gifts. The temple didn't have ushers, television technicians, lighting technicians, or structural engineers, as we have in some of our churches today; but you better believe everyone in that group of 822 had a very important job.

There's a third group. Verses 15 and 16 tell us of the Levites and the "leaders of Levites, who were *in charge of the outside work of the house of God.*" In those days, "outside work" didn't just mean those who landscaped the temple grounds. Verse 16 refers to the leaders who worked outside of the house of God, those who judged, handled civil affairs, and counseled and ministered to the public away from the place of worship. You probably can't remember *one* of their names! It's almost as if God has said, "I don't want you to remember those names." They are like those small white crosses in the cemetery. We do not remember them individually but rather as a mass of willing workers who made it possible for important things to go right on without a hitch.

Not a business today could exist for long without those extra-effort "nobodies" who diligently labor away from the limelight. There are many: the secretary who handles endless details; the custodian who keeps the place clean and neat; the personnel manager who interviews new people, listens to complaints, and keeps peace within the ranks; and the technicians and inspectors who work in rooms without windows to make sure a product is up to snuff.

A fourth "willing unknown" is revealed in verse 17: "Mattaniah [his genealogy follows] . . . was the leader in beginning the thanksgiving at *prayer*" (italics added). You probably didn't even know Mattaniah ever existed! But God says he was a leader. Where? On his knees. Was that important? Believe it or not, he was a major cause for the success of the temple. He probably couldn't preach his way out of a paper bag; but, wow, could he pray! As it has always been, the unsung hero of the church of Jesus Christ is the kneeling saint.

Have you ever been in touch with a prayer warrior? If you haven't you have missed out on a great joy. I was in contact with one in Houston years ago when I first became serious about the ministry. I had the delightful privilege of being put on her prayer list. She was an unusual kind of a woman. She could quote chapters of Isaiah with ease. Great chunks of Scripture came from her lips. She was either in the Book or on her knees. But few people in her church even knew she was around.

This prayer warrior prayed me through seminary. Later she upheld me during my first experience in the gospel ministry. She supported my wife and me through the births of our four children and through the valleys as well as the peaks of our lives. But most people who know me know nothing of this "willing unknown"— the *Mattaniah* of my life—who poured out her soul that God might use me for His glory.

That's what this fellow in Nehemiah 11:17 was known for. He prayed.

Finally, Nehemiah 11:22 tells us about the fifth unknown: an overseer of the Levites in Jerusalem whose name was Uzzi. Uzzi? Never in my life have I known an Uzzi! What did he do? Well, he was from the sons of Asaph—*the singers for the services of the house of God. The Living Bible* says that the sons of Asaph were the "clan" that became the tabernacle singers. What a tremendous thing! These people willingly sang for the glory of God.

Do you remember these unknowns: (1) the people who willingly moved into the city; (2) the people who worked in the temple; (3) the people who worked outside in related areas; (4) the people who willingly prayed; and (5) the people who sang in the services for God? All of them willingly gave their services.

My Favorite Anonymous People

As I write these words, my mind is flooded with the faces of those who work behind the scenes so that my leadership might not get bogged down: my wife at home who faithfully and consistently supports me, encourages me, works with our children, and takes up the slack—all without any glory; my staff at church who stick with it day in and day out; the board members and officers who fill strategic roles yet hold down full-time employment; the people who play instruments and sing in choirs in multiple services Sunday after Sunday; the people who pray, who help in the nursery, who teach, who work in our library, who give, who counsel, who visit; gifted technicians who voluntarily handle the sound system, the television monitors, the lighting, and the tape recordings of every message. There are others who help with parking, maintenance, and a host of other volunteer tasks. Without them, my life would be reduced to tedious, endless details that would become the enemy of my ministry. I give God praise for each one of them who willingly stands behind me without the benefit of public applause. With profound gratitude, I freely declare their significance.

I am occasionally asked, "Who is your favorite Bible character?" I suppose most people expect me to say David or Elijah or Paul or Moses. I usually surprise them with a group of names like Jabez, Amos, Enoch, Mephibosheth, Epaphroditus, Onesiphorus, and (of course) Habakkuk. They stare at me as if I've spoken in a foreign language! But those really are among my favorites. They all were great men and marvelous believers! But they also were virtually unheard-of, anonymous individuals. Each one, however, was a great leader.

Timeless Truths

We've spent considerable time dealing with many "willing unknowns." Now, putting all of it together, allow me to share some timeless truths with you. The first one is this: *Your gifts make you valuable although not necessarily famous.* If you are gifted in an area that will never reach the spotlight, don't worry about it. You are as valuable as Mattaniah or Uzzi, and you will be just about as well-known. But relax; you are not anonymous to God. That fact introduces the second truth: *Every labor done in love is remembered by God.* It's never forgotten. Take note of Hebrews 6:10:

> For God is not unjust so as to forget your work and the love which you have shown toward His name, in having ministered and in still ministering to the saints.

Put Hebrews 6:10 in the margin of your mind and every time you begin to feel sorry because you are not in the limelight, remember that God never overlooks one deed.

The third truth that I see in Nehemiah 11 is: *Our final rewards will be determined on the basis of faithfulness—not public applause.* The public may never know of your ministry, but that will have nothing to do with final rewards. God never checks an applause meter to determine our rewards.

Quite late in the evening that same day when all of us had seen the military cemetery in California, the scene of those white crosses passed in review in my memory. I thought, "The dead have not died in vain. They still speak." And I realized anew how important it is to honor the large number of people who, though unknown, still minister that a few might lead.

John McCrae closed his immortal poem with the reminder:

> To you from failing hands we throw the torch.
> Be yours to hold it high.
> If ye break faith with us who die
> We shall not sleep, though poppies blow
> In Flanders fields.

May God genuinely encourage and stimulate every "willing unknown" who reads these words. And by the way, the poet knew what he was writing about. Lt. Col. John McCrae's body lies in Flanders fields.

Unknown, but not forgotten.

14

Happiness Is on the Wall

If happiness were a disease, none other would be more contagious. If you laugh often, if you're having fun in life, if you're never very far from a smile, you'll have no trouble infecting people and making friends. People who really enjoy life are always, *always* in demand. They are unbelievably infectious!

Teachers who are happy and carry out their teaching in a winsome way have no trouble getting students to line up for their courses. When a salesman is genuinely happy, he gets writer's cramp filling out orders. When a service station manager has happiness, a steady stream of cars will pour in. When a college president is happy, the public relations department has an easier job. When the owner and waitresses of a restaurant are friendly and happy, the word spreads. Why? Because happiness is a rare commodity. In fact, it's almost extinct. If you question that, check out the drivers next time you're on the freeway. Every one of them looks as if he could eat corn out of a Coke bottle. Even at a funeral you won't see faces that long.

I suppose it's understandable. Our economic scene does not promote happiness. Homes and property have never been more expensive. The promises of tomorrow have never been more bleak than at this present hour. There is an international famine that seems to be spreading. The crime rate has come to an all-time high. Illegitimacy, rape, pornography, child-battering, drug abuse, political scandals, malpractice charges, marital infidelity, energy and ecological crises add heavy weights to the thin wires of our sanity.

Someone has dubbed our time "the aspirin age," a quite accurate description. Hospitals have never been more expensive or overcrowded. It is a documented fact that over half of those occupying hospital beds are there because of mental or emotional disorders.[25]

People in health care professions are also extremely alarmed over the growing suicide rate. It is now one of the major causes of death. Even the young cannot cope. Suicide is the number two cause of death among young adults.[26]

Add to these woes the ingredients of discouragement, the epidemic of divorce, and the breakdown of child training. Mix into that the problems connected with our religious scene, the international tensions as they relate to Israel and the Arab states—not to mention the turmoil in Africa and the threat of Red China—and you begin to doubt the familiar words: "Laugh and the world laughs with you; weep and you weep alone." It seems rather that the one who laughs, laughs *alone*. Every day seems to bring a surprise attack from Darth Vader, the representative of evil in *Star Wars*.

Yet in spite of our current situation, God wants to set our hearts right concerning our day and age. I'm convinced He still wants His children happy. He can use the twelfth chapter of Nehemiah to teach us His principles on happiness. In the days of Nehemiah the people faced many depressing circumstances. They were, in fact, plagued with the most difficult times imaginable. There was nothing to lend their hearts toward rejoicing. Nevertheless, they were filled with joy and laughter.

I don't mean that we should become like the proverbial ostriches who stick their heads in the sand and blindly smile their way through hard times. But I am convinced that Nehemiah 12 will help to lighten our load as we see things more from God's perspective. I believe that we are marching toward the culmination of His divine plan—regardless of the scars we must now bear on our wounded earth. If we can catch God's thoughts and see life as He sees it, the friction of living will be lessened.

Leaders need to be happy people! Those who look to a leader for encouragement and hope aren't ready for a personification of the grim reaper. Many of the followers crawl to work every morning whipped black-and-blue by domestic conflicts and a ton of financial worries. They face a day of monotonous demands and thankless tasks, only later to return home to bickering, discontented mates and kids. Away from the job they have little more to look forward to than the glare of a television set. Somewhere, somehow, God can use you to introduce the one ingredient—real and lasting joy—that will lighten their load.

Gathering The Right Leaders

In Nehemiah 12:27, the people have gathered to dedicate the recently completed wall. The city is slowly beginning to show signs of progress—new homes, new businesses, the whole gamut of urban renewal. Although times were still hard, there was a new spark of enthusiasm, a renewed vision—even though there was much left to do. But the wall was finished: broad, stable, strong, well-constructed, and well-engineered. The wall was the main attraction. Having moved into the city and having begun to build their own homes, the citizens decided to dedicate this project to God.

The dedication of the wall is the obvious subject of Nehemiah 12:27–47. However, we find much more than that. We find a people whose hearts were really rejoicing. They were happy! Even though they had left suburbia and had to scrounge to find materials to build their urban dwellings, they were really joyful because their eyes were on the Lord:

> Now at the dedication of the wall of Jerusalem they sought out the Levites from all their places, to bring them to Jerusalem so that they might celebrate the dedication with gladness, with hymns of thanksgiving and with songs to the accompaniment of cymbals, harps, and lyres. So the sons of the singers were assembled from the district around Jerusalem (vv. 27,28).

The Hebrew word for *gladness* means "gaiety, mirth, pleasure, delight." The people brought in this group of specialists and said,

"Lead us in a happy celebration! Let's have fun!" Then they added to the celebration by singing hymns and songs accompanied by cymbals, harps, and lyres. This was quite a combo! I suppose they could have named it "Nehemiah's Ragtime Band."

People from all around were selected to lead in the celebration of joy. It was designed to be an unforgettable, enjoyable day.

Clean Up Your Act!

The dedication consisted of more fun and games, however. Notice something very important in verse 30: "And the priests and the Levites purified themselves; they also purified the people, the gates, and the wall." It must not be overlooked that before there was one moment of celebration, purification occurred.

We're not told exactly what was meant by "purification," but it no doubt had to do with personal cleansing through a sin offering. In order to carry on the celebration of the wall, their hearts had to be pure. We too need to remember that to minister to other people, our hearts must be clean before God. Holiness precedes happiness.

That's a good point to emphasize with anybody who leads. The first step to a happy countenance is a clean heart. And there isn't a leader reading my words who hasn't tried to fake a clean heart and failed. Moral carelessness and borderline sin give laughter a hollow ring. Mark it down, there can be no tolerance of evil, no laughing off of the things God hates. Any leader who expects his efforts to lift the spirits of others must start with purification.

Everybody On The Wall!

Let's move ahead to the first procedure in the dedication ceremonies: "Then I [Nehemiah] had the leaders of Judah come up on the top of the wall and I appointed two great choirs" (v. 31). Picture that! Maybe a ladder leaned on the wall and Nehemiah yelled, "Come on up, everybody on the wall!" And up they came by the dozens onto this great broad wall that went around Jerusalem. Verse 31 tells us that the first great choir proceeded to Nehemiah's right, on top of the wall, toward the gate down at the bottom of the city, the Refuse Gate. Then verse 38 informs us: "The second choir proceeded to the left, while I [Nehemiah] followed them with half of the people on the wall." Ezra was in the first choir, and Nehemiah linked himself with the second choir; so we have Ezra on one side of the city's wall and Nehemiah on the other side. I've often tried to get a mental picture of what that scene must have looked like from outside the wall. What a blast they must have had! Hundreds of singers, all sorts of instruments, a spirit of hilarity that certainly wouldn't resemble today's average church service! It probably looked more like a bunny hop line in the 1950s. That's what I get when I picture verse 43 in my mind:

> And on that day [the day of happy celebration, the day of dedication] they offered great sacrifices and rejoiced because God had given them great joy, even the women and children rejoiced. . . .

You'll never convince me that all those women and kids stood at ramrod-straight attention and walked in step like pallbearers, tight-lipped and straitlaced. No, they got with it! It was sort of like a Jewish Disneyland parade, if I read this correctly. From a distance I'd guess they resembled a charismatic drum and bugle corps led by some guys that looked like the Three Stooges in Salvation Army uniforms.

And they were loud! Verse 43 concludes, "the joy of Jerusalem was heard from afar." We've all arrived late to a football game and heard the yelling, the band playing, the growing crescendo of the roar of thousands, and had our hearts pound with excitement. This was like that. And in the middle of it all were Nehemiah, Ezra, and the other leaders having a wonderful time. What a delightful day to remember!

Needed: Smiling, Singing Saints

Remember the words in Proverbs 17:22: "a joyful heart is good medicine"? Well, there's another verse you may not have found which states, "A joyful heart makes a cheerful face, but when the heart is sad, the spirit is broken" (Prov. 15:13). Isn't that the truth! It's the individual who smiles and sings his way through life whom people want to be around. I repeat, a joyful heart is contagious. And it fits any scene, no matter how bad the circumstances.

When I was in seminary, Cynthia and I lived in one of the campus apartments. What a dump! My study was so small that I had to step outside to turn a page. We had hot and cold running rats. (I'm happy to say those apartments have all been destroyed.) There were enough crummy surroundings to depress even Norman Vincent Peale. But we were determined we would cultivate our sense of humor instead of letting the place paralyze us.

Looking back, some of our most pleasant memories occurred there. We entertained faculty members, fixed exotic meals (all with hamburger!), and even sang duets with the couple next door. The walls were so paper thin that in the morning I used to harmonize with my neighbor as I showered.

How about you? Have you stopped singing, or stopped smiling?

When you sing, your kids will sing too. And they won't care where they are! Some time ago, I took little Chuckie, our youngest, to a grocery store with me. We came up to the check-out stand to purchase a few items. For some reason, the store was abnormally quiet. Chuckie, who was sitting in the cart, reached over and grabbed a handful of mints. While he was trying to unwrap one of them he began to sing in a loud voice, "Jesus loves me this I know [everybody kind of stared at him], for the Bible tells me so. Little ones . . ." He sang softer as he realized a dozen eyes were on him.

"Go ahead—'to Him belong,'" a young woman said to Chuckie. Then she turned to me: "Do you know Christ as your Savior?"

"Why, yes I do," I answered.

"I've been a Christian about a year and a half," she said.

"Isn't that interesting," I said. "My son led us into an opportunity to encourage each other."

I also found out that the checker (who also had stopped to listen) was disturbed with a broken marriage. Chuckie had just come bursting out with a song at precisely the right moment. His happy heart soothed the hurt of another.

Don't stop singing! Sing this afternoon. Sing on your way home from work! One of the most exuberant expressions of a happy heart is a singing mouth. (Glance at Ephesians 5:18,19.)

I'm impressed with the fact that Nehemiah 12:43 does not say the song was heard from afar. It says, "the *joy* was heard from afar" (italics added). That encourages me! People don't hear the lips and the words, they hear the joy of the heart. Most people are so lonely, so empty. If they see you and witness within you a joyful spirit, they don't say, "Oh, you sing tenor." Or, "Hey, I learned that song some time ago." No, that's not the way it is. People are starved for happiness. When it's expressed in any authentic manner, they are greatly encouraged.

The Secret: The Right Focus

One great application pours out of these verses: *Happiness is not dependent on outward circumstances but upon inward focus.* When you have focused correctly, you can smile and sing through an experience and come out rejoicing. It all depends on your inward focus.

My closing comments in this chapter go back to those of you who are now in leadership positions or plan to be in the future.

- Do you bring joy to those you lead?
- Is your leadership marked by a good sense of humor?

I know of few things more magnetic than a smile or a cheerful disposition, especially among those in God's work. How easy it is to become intense, severe, and even oppressive! The people under Nehemiah's leadership felt free to rejoice and laugh. Do the people who are under your leadership feel that freedom? How about your children?

I understand that Charles Haddon Spurgeon was once chided for injecting a fair amount of humor into his preaching. With a twinkle in his eye, he replied, "If only you knew how much I hold back, you would commend me."

The Jews laughed on the wall as they rejoiced over God's provision. They sang together, and their joy flooded the hillside so all could hear and be glad. Had their circumstances changed? No, *they* had changed.

Have you?

15
Taking Problems
by the Throat

The life of Ludwig van Beethoven, although one of great ecstasy, was also checkered with sporadic agony. By the age of five, Beethoven was playing the violin under the tutelage of his father—also an accomplished musician. By the time he was thirteen, Beethoven was a concert organist. In his twenties he was already studying under the very watchful eyes of Haydn and Mozart. In fact, Mozart spoke prophetic words when he declared that Beethoven would give the world something worth listening to by the time his life ended.

As Beethoven began to develop his skills, he became a prolific composer. During his lifetime, he wrote nine majestic symphonies and five concertos for piano, not to mention numerous pieces of chamber music. Ludwig van Beethoven also wrote sonatas and pieces for violin and piano. He has thrilled us with the masterful works of unique harmony that broke with the traditions of his times. The man was a genius.

Beethoven was not, however, a stranger to difficulties. During his twenties, he began to lose his hearing. His fingers "became thick," he said on one occasion. He couldn't *feel* the music as he once had. His hearing problem haunted him in the middle years of his life, but he kept it a well-guarded secret. When he reached his fifties, Beethoven was stone deaf. Three years later he made a tragic attempt to conduct an orchestra and failed miserably. Approximately five years later, he died during a fierce thunder storm.

He was deaf, yet a magnificent musician. On one occasion, Beethoven was overheard shouting at the top of his voice as he slammed both fists on the keyboard, "I will take life by the throat!" He had determined not to give in. Many of his biographers feel that because of his great determination, Beethoven remained far more productive than he otherwise would have been. Indeed, he took life by the throat.

I would like to borrow that phrase and apply it to leadership. I won't tarry on such things as physical infirmity, though some of us today may wrestle with similar maladies—perhaps secrets known only by you and God. I will apply Beethoven's phrase to the areas of wrong that we must face and "take by the throat." Our main character will not be Beethoven, but rather Nehemiah and the final chapter of his book.

At this point, Nehemiah was confronted with four great problems that he "took by the throat." He was determined not to let them conquer him or the people he served.

There is a verse tucked away in Romans that says "These things that were written in the Scriptures so long ago are to teach us patience and to encourage us . . . (Rom. 15:4, TLB). I want us to find encouragement and instruction from the study of this great passage, Nehemiah 13.

Understanding the Background

For a period of time following the dedication of the wall, Nehemiah continued to establish a righteous government in Jerusalem. Eventually, we learn in verse 6, he left the city and went back to his first assignment as a cupbearer to the king. We also become aware that certain things took place while he was gone:

> But during all this time [that is, the time described in verses 1–5] I was not in Jerusalem, for in the thirty-second year of Artaxerxes king of Babylon I had gone to the king. After some time, however, I asked leave from the king.

We don't know how long Nehemiah was absent from Jerusalem. But while the cat was away, the mice did play in that city! When he returned to the city, Nehemiah discovered four great areas of wrong. When he encountered these "problems," he took them by the throat.

Compromising Companionship

The first problem is revealed in Nehemiah 13:4–9 and it is what I'll label *the problem of a compromising companionship*. To appreciate it, you have to understand the main characters involved. Verse 5 introduces them to us.

Prior to Nehemiah's return, Eliashib (the priest who was appointed over the chambers of the house of God and who was a relative of Tobiah) had prepared a large room for Tobiah. We do not know much about these two men. Later on, Eliashib is called "the high priest." He was responsible for the vessels, the rooms, and the worship in the house of God. Eliashib had planned to set aside part of a chamber in the house of God to house Tobiah.

Tobiah, as recorded in the book, had been an enemy of God and a thorn in Nehemiah's side. Nehemiah had faced him repeatedly as Tobiah had tried to stop construction of the wall and had personally criticized, attacked, and assaulted Nehemiah. But all the way through his Jerusalem project, Nehemiah made sure that Tobiah never got inside the walls. Tobiah is the classic example of the rebellious unbeliever or the carnal Christian who tries every way in the world to thwart the work of God.

However, while Nehemiah was away Eliashib had said, "Let's prepare a room for Tobiah" (Neh. 13:5). You see, in those days, the house of God was different from the church of today. It was joined by chambers—large rooms that often held grain or utensils or vessels of worship. So Eliashib had said, "Let's clear out the area normally given to this storage and provide a nice room for Tobiah. Let's bring him in. He has been rejected long enough. Let's put him into the courts, or into the chambers." If I read this correctly, verse 9 suggests that he had a suite of rooms: "I gave an order and they cleansed the rooms." (Notice the plural.) Now back to the story:

> Eliashib the priest, who was appointed over the chambers of the house of our God, being related to Tobiah, had prepared a large

— 169 —

room for him, where formerly they put the grain of offerings (vv. 4,5).

The remainder of verse 5 describes the rooms. In the next verse Nehemiah explains that he had been away. Then in verse 7, he says, "I came to Jerusalem and learned about the evil that Eliashib had done for Tobiah." In short, Nehemiah came back to Jerusalem and found that the house of God had been infiltrated by Tobiah and his evil plans. What did Nehemiah do about it? He took the problem by the throat!

Verse 8 says: "It was very displeasing to me. . . ." Nehemiah was careful to give us, first of all, his attitude toward evil before he told us the action that he was to take against it. "I threw all of Tobiah's household goods out of the room" (v. 8).

It's remarkable how practical—even earthy—God's Word can be! People who envision these saints of the Old Testament with halos, untarnished robes, and well-polished sandals have missed the whole point of the narrative. Nehemiah went into the rooms and began to throw all of Tobiah's gear out into the streets. It was a spring housecleaning! Having Tobiah in the house of God was like having a possum in the chicken coop. Or having Tobiah present in the temple was like having a bust of Luther in the Vatican!

Tobiah had no reason to be in the house of God. I love verse 9 because it's so vivid. "Then I gave an order and they cleansed the rooms." They fumigated that place. Nehemiah didn't want even the smell of Tobiah to hang around the building of God.

Isn't it interesting that we really don't know how to get mad about the right things. Too often we jump and scream about the wrong things. Now, you'll never convince me in a thousand years that Nehemiah folded his hands and said, "Tsk, tsk, now that is a shame. We must pray about what we should do with Tobiah's belongings." No! He opened that door and said, "Haul that stuff out!" They carried out Tobiah's belongings, and when the room was stripped clean, swept out, and ready, they brought in the grain (see verse 9). Can you imagine Tobiah coming home that night to a room full of grain?

Nehemiah did that because he was determined he would not live with *wrong* (Tobiah's evil) in a place that was built for *right*. Some people still have not become convinced of that. God's leader must constantly guard against compromise.

Our companions do help determine our character; we become like those we spend time with. Do you have any idea of the effect your friends are having on your life? I have lost count of the parents who have said to me, "You know, it all started with the wrong friendship." Many men have shared with me, "You know, it all started when I allowed this individual to have an impact on my life. It tore me down."

Nehemiah didn't tolerate the evil; he took the problem by the throat. He reminds me of Daniel. Remember the time the king told Daniel to bow down and worship the image or he'd be killed and thrown in with the lions? Daniel didn't bow down and worship the image. He went back to his room and prayed. They hated him for that, and so they accused him and put him in the lions' den. We know that God protected Daniel from the lions, but I also think those cats didn't snack on Daniel because he was three-fourths gristle and one-fourth backbone. He was a man of conviction.

In so many words, Nehemiah said, "I don't care if it means losing votes as governor. I'm not interested in a popularity contest. I'm interested in cleansing the evil that's in the house of God."

Financial Fiasco

The next problem Nehemiah faced (revealed in Nehemiah 13:10–14) I'll call *the problem of a financial fiasco*. I like the way verse 10 begins: "I also discovered." That tells me that he was looking. A leader keeps his eyes open! A great leader doesn't walk around whistling "Dixie" with his mind in neutral. He listens. He looks.

Most wise parents I know are always looking at and listening to what their kids are doing. They listen carefully to the music that comes from each room, and they find out what's going on behind any door that stays closed.

Nehemiah discovered something that was wrong.

> The portions of the Levites had not been given them [the Levites], so that the Levites and the singers who performed the service had gone away, each to his own field (Neh. 13:10).

What does that mean?

In those days the people who served in the temple were called Levites and drew their living from the temple. People who sang there were supported by the people who attended. People who ministered derived their income from the paying of the tithe.

But in those days, as is true even now, there was selfishness in the area of money. Nehemiah returned to Jerusalem and found that the singers and the Levites were living in the suburbs. They were supposed to live in the temple and receive their income from their temple duties. But no money was coming in. At least that is what is implied here. Did Nehemiah say "My! This is something we ought to discuss in a committee meeting." Not at all! We read in verse 11: "I reprimanded the officials." Although he was losing more and more votes at the polls, Nehemiah was persistent. He continued to say, "This is wrong. God requires in the law a paying of the tithe, and you're not doing it."

So Nehemiah pulled together the men who were officials and he said, "'Why is the house of God forsaken?' Then I gathered them together and restored them to their posts" (v. 11). I suspect Nehemiah even raised his voice in this verbal rebuke to the officials. He said, in effect, "This has no place in the life of God's people!" And then he suggested a plan of change and immediately put it into operation.

Finally, in verse 14, he prayed, "Remember me for this, O my God, and do not blot out my loyal deeds which I have performed for the house of my God and its services."

I firmly believe that there is a great place for prayer. I believe there are certain problems in life for which only prayer will provide the answer. But when there are situations that result from direct disobedience to what God has said in His Word, prayer can become a spiritual cop-out. *Obedience is needed.*

If your small child runs into the street when a truck is coming, you don't fall on your knees and pray that the child will be preserved. You do everything in your power to snatch the child from the path of the truck, even if it means hurting yourself.

There are times when we traffic in the realm of wrong When this occurs, God does not expect His child to fall to his knees and offer long confessions or petitions. God says, in effect, "Get off your knees and go about the business of correcting the wrong." This is what I find in the story of Nehemiah. And it is applicable for today. It's all part of taking problems by the throat.

Some of you may need to take a long look at what God's Word teaches about giving. You may need to carefully evaluate just what part God is playing in your giving plans. If you were to compile a list of things that are part of your expenditures, where would the Lord's part be? Would it be toward the bottom or toward the top? Shouldn't his part be *first?* All that we are and all that we have and hope to be comes down from His gracious hands. A grateful Christian is a giving Christian.

Secularized Sabbath

There is a third problem reported in verses 15–22 which Nehemiah grabbed by the throat. I will call it *the problem of the secularized Sabbath*. Look at verse 15:

> In those days I saw in Judah some who were trading wine presses on the sabbath, and bringing in sacks of grain and loading them on donkeys, as well as wine, grapes, figs, and all kinds of loads, and they brought them into Jerusalem on the sabbath day.

We must understand here that the Sabbath day has never been and never will be Sunday. In the Jewish system the Sabbath was Saturday, the day of rest. It was an observance of the day that our wonderful Creator God set aside for rest during His creative week.

Remember that covenantal promise the people made to God in Nehemiah 10:31?

> As for the peoples of the land who bring wares or any grain on the sabbath day to sell, we will not buy from them on the sabbath or a holy day; and we will forgo the crops the seventh year and the exaction of every debt.

In other words, the people said they would observe—to the letter—a spiritual day of rest.

Nehemiah was walking through the city, and he saw that the merchants were back at their old tricks. The grain was still being sold on the Sabbath. Loads were being brought in through the gates and taken back out. There were profit making, expenditures of monies, and the receiving of goods—all on the Sabbath. Nehemiah must have shaken his head in disappointment. The promise was still fresh in his memory.

> So I admonished them on the day they sold food. Also men of Tyre were living there who imported fish and all kinds of merchandise, and sold them to the sons of Judah on the sabbath, even in Jerusalem (vv. 15,16).

There's nothing wrong with making a profit and nothing at all wrong with having a good business—even if it is a fish business. Just *don't* do it under the Jewish economy on the Sabbath.

What did Nehemiah do about the problem? Did he just shake his head and passively say, "Guys, we really need to do something about this!" No he took it by the throat!

> Then I reprimanded the nobles of Judah and said to them, "What is this evil thing you are doing, by profaning the sabbath day? . . ."
> And it came about that just as it grew dark at the gates of Jerusalem before the sabbath (vv. 17,19).

This means it was Friday evening at sundown, because in Nehemiah's lifetime the day was measured from six o'clock in the evening until six o'clock on the following evening. So the Sabbath ran, by our time, from 6:00 P.M. Friday until 6:00 P.M. Saturday.

Nehemiah observed the sun beginning to set and said, "Shut the gates. The sabbath is coming." In verse 19, we read: "I commanded that the doors should be shut and that they should not open them until after the sabbath."

Did Nehemiah leave it at that? No way! He must have said to himself, "Merchants have a way of picking locks; they can get right through those gates. We've got to watch those guys—not all of them, but some of them." The verse goes on to say, "Then I stationed some of my servants at the gates that no load should enter on the sabbath day."

I love the next two verses: "Once or twice the traders and merchants of every kind of merchandise spent the night outside Jerusalem" (v. 20). Do you think Nehemiah won many friends among those fellows who had fish outside the gate of Jerusalem and were waiting to bring their product in? Do you think that bothered him? Take a look at verse 21: "Then I warned them and said to them, "Why do you spend the night in front of the wall? If you do so again, I will use force against you.'" What Nehemiah said, in our vernacular, is, "If you do that again, I'll take you on. I'll punch your lights out!" And his warning had its effect! The verse concludes with these words: "From that time on they did not come on the sabbath."

An aggressive plan worked! Nehemiah knew what to get mad about. He knew where he stood on the issue of a *secularized Sabbath,* and he held his ground. Nehemiah said, "Don't come back on the Sabbath. Saturday is the day we honor our God."

You may have a conviction God has given you. My Christian friend, if this is the case, you had better carry it out. You'd better have the grit that is necessary to say, "No, I will not" or, "Yes, I will continue" because there will always be individuals who will try to change your standards to fit theirs. The answer for you is to take the problem by the throat.

For example, I know of an outstanding Christian educator who has just taken over the presidency of one of the most humanistically oriented colleges in the nation. On the day of his major interview for the position, he made it very clear that should his responsibilities on the job interfere with his prior commitment to Christ and His kingdom, then the ethic of the latter would win out. He stated his case honestly, and he got the job. How we need more men of similar conviction!

By the way, let me pause a moment to add this thought: I have never known anyone who uprooted a deep-seated wrong without first becoming sufficiently angry. Anger can stir up motivation. We need to declare an all-out war against wrong in our personal lives. Anything less than that won't work.

Domestic Disobedience

There is a fourth problem with which Nehemiah was confronted. Perhaps this particular issue hits harder than any of the other three as we find Nehemiah, once again, declaring war against a wrong. In this instance, there is *the problem of domestic disobedience.* Nehemiah 13:23 says; "In those days I also saw that the Jews had married women from Ashdod, Ammon, and Moab."

The Jews were supposed to refrain from intermarriage in order to maintain the solidarity of their race. Besides that, interracial marriage had brought tragic results on the children. Verse 24 reveals Nehemiah's concern for the children as well as those involved in these marriages: "As for their children, half spoke in the language of Ashdod, and none of them was able to speak the language of Judah." Hebrew was the language of the Scripture, by the way, and so they could glean nothing from the Scripture. The children were able to speak only the language of their own people. So Nehemiah had a mixed multitude, a result of the intermingling of languages and customs. What did he do? Are you ready for this? Nehemiah said (v. 25), "So I contended with them and cursed them. . . ." This does not mean he used profanity. Rather, it means "to be disrespectful, to dishonor." It's a severe term, implying "to treat with contempt, to revile." Then the verse says he "struck some of them and pulled out their hair." That's a strong reaction! The Hebrew word, which is translated *pulled out their hair* means originally "to make bald, to make slick or polished." It referred mainly to the beard, a plucking out of part of the beard. Nehemiah was so indignant over the wrongdoing of these Jews that he literally ran around yanking out their hair. I don't think he took delight in jerking out people's beards and pulling hair from their heads, but this action was indicative of the emotional intensity Nehemiah felt as he lost himself in the pursuit of right.

We are so careful, so tender, so tactful. Too much so! We are afraid to confront. Our lives skate along, glazed with compromise and toleration. Often at the heart of a compounded, complex matter, we're afraid to say honestly to someone, "You know something? You never did take care of that issue back there, did you?" Or, "You know what? Selfishness is at the heart of the problem you're wrestling with." Nehemiah was not afraid to pluck out beards for the sake of right. He *literally* took that problem by the throat!

God says to you about something in the realm of your domestic life, "This is wrong. Do something about it." Your personal life is so important to God that He longs to maintain His control over you. If you are careless, all sorts of "Tobiahs," such as, "financial selfishness" will infiltrate your life. All those areas of rest God wants to give you, you will fill up with worry and you will secularize the spiritual Sabbath. By and by, these things will affect your entire life.

In the last verses of Nehemiah's "memoirs," he comes before God in prayer, saying, "Remember me, my God. I have only their good at heart."

Overcoming Passivity

While attending a conference years ago, I was impressed with a statement made by Dr. Art Glasser: "Passivity is an enemy."

These words have rung in my ears for almost twenty years. As I try to express Nehemiah's closing message to leaders, that statement seems to say it best. No leader dare play with wrong. It must be taken by the throat. Passivity is an enemy.

Look at how Nehemiah took passivity by the throat:

1. *Nehemiah faced the wrong head-on.* I've never known a wrong to be solved until it is admitted to be just that—a wrong. When Nehemiah learned of wrong, he faced the situation head-on. If you have a problem in your church, your business, your home— anywhere in your life—face it head-on. Don't skirt it. Sure, it will be painful, but deal with it. Start today.

2. *Nehemiah dealt with the wrong severely.* After seeing the wrong or the problem as it really was, he dealt with it severely. I'm sure some people said, "Man, Nehemiah, you're getting cranky. You used to smile a lot more than you do now. I'm not voting for you for governor next time." And I'm just as sure that Nehemiah must have thought, "I don't care. I answer to God!" Our lives must not be politically swayed by the applause of the public. That's really difficult because it's hard to stand against wrong and not appear to be a crotchety old crank. But Nehemiah stood firm. He didn't pick a fight; he just dealt with sin severely. Any leader who expects to be respected must do the same.

3. *Nehemiah worked toward a permanent correction.* It's not

enough just to condemn the wrong. You must do something to replace it. I'm thrilled with the way God communicates this in the Bible. Whenever God says, "Don't do this," He backs it up with, "Do that instead." God always balances a negative with a positive. So it must be in our lives. When you take some wrong by the throat and plan to get rid of it, something better must take its place.

4. *Nehemiah always followed up the wrong with prayer.* When Nehemiah had done all that he could, he fell before God and said, "Oh, God, bless every one of these efforts. Give me direction and more wisdom and guidance. Remember me as I have done all I can to correct the wrong. Honor Yourself as I stand alone."

Honesty . . . Conviction . . . Devotion

Three brief applications form Nehemiah's final counsel to leaders.

First, *taking any problem by the throat starts with an honest observation.* Detection always precedes solution. You can never solve a problem you cannot define. You must define it, call a spade a spade. The problem may be a compromising alliance that you have begun—in your business, in your social life, or in your dating life. Maybe you've begin to let go of the reins of responsibility. Whatever the wrong in your life may be, it's bound to take its toll on you.

Do you remember Samson? He walked so far away from God that when God's Spirit finally departed from him, Samson didn't even know it. The King James Version says, "He wist not that the Lord was departed from him" (Judg. 16:20). He didn't even know that God had left! Samson had lived a lie so long and his leadership was so dishonest that he failed to see the full impact of his hypocrisy.

Honest observation must come first.

Second, *the honest observation must be matched with courageous conviction.* Any leader who determines to live a godly life is going to have to brace himself with conviction. A godly walk requires a fearless determination and the taking of strong measures to stand firm.

In the spiritual realm we cannot tolerate everybody doing his own thing. If we do, our Christian conviction weakens. I'm not saying we should never bend. I'm not advocating blind intolerance. I am saying that it is the responsibility of Christian leaders to stand firm in spite of those who don't agree. You will never be popular if you do that, especially with those who don't like the way you're laying the bricks.

Joshua said, "Choose for yourselves today whom you will serve" (Josh. 24:15). Notice he didn't say, "Shall we discuss this idea? Would you like to talk it over?" He said, "That's it!" A leader must declare his convictions.

Third, *honest observation and courageous conviction must be tempered with deep devotion.* This is where many well-meaning Christians miss it. They become spiritual headhunters: negative, angry, witch-hunting Christians who are always suspicious and often fighting. Their joy of the Lord is replaced with a long, deep frown. The leader must maintain a balance between standing for the truth and keeping his heart warm before the Lord.

I think it is significant that the final scene in Nehemiah's book portrays him on his knees asking God for grace. He had fought hard for the right, but he had kept his heart soft before the Lord. What a magnificent model of leadership! He was a man of honesty, conviction, and devotion.

Our world is filled with a fearful and confused humanity. Shepherdless sheep by the millions long for a voice of assurance, a cause to believe in, an authentic model to follow. They cry out for someone to calm their fears, to solve their confusion, to channel their energies. They are calling for leaders.

Can you handle another brick?

Study Guide

Chapter 1

The Matter at Hand

1. Maybe you've come to the end of this first chapter thinking, "This book isn't for me. I'm no leader! I'm just an ordinary person."

   But are you sure about that? Maybe you're not trying to reorganize a whole city, or even plan a neighborhood party. But when it comes right down to it, all leadership is simply influence. Now you can't say you don't influence anyone! Think about it for a moment. Over whom do you have the greatest influence . . . your children? Co-workers? Friends? Don't skip this question, because it will make a difference in how you apply the content of this book.

   In this book, an ancient man by the name of Nehemiah is going to hand you a few bricks, bricks you can use to build a character of such quality that your faith can't be destroyed. But those bricks of character also make good bricks of leadership— qualities you can use to guide the people around you.

   Remember, a great leader doesn't have to be someone who's

well known. A great leader is just an ordinary person who is highly motivated. And that can be you!

2.   In the days of Nehemiah, a city's wall was its most crucial structure because it meant protection from attack. As Christians, we need to have walls in place around our hearts to protect us from the invasions of our enemy, Satan.

What kinds of weapons do you think Satan uses to batter against your walls? What do you think your heart would be like if he succeeded in gaining an entry?

In light of your answers, what kinds of bricks do you think would be most effective to have in your protective wall? Think in terms of character qualities and disciplines.

3.   You have some idea now of what a strong wall might look like. Take an inspection tour of the wall around your own heart. Are there bricks that need replacing or maybe sections that have crumbled altogether? Identify some of the weaker areas so you can concentrate on them as we move on in our study of Nehemiah's example.

Chapter 2

A Leader—From the Knees Up!

1.   Reread the story of Eli in 1 Samuel 3. God's displeasure over the situation is obvious, but can you figure out where Eli went wrong? For some clues, refer to the four marks of a competent leader we read about in this chapter.

Think back to our study of the first chapter. Who was it you said you were leading? Take a look at their lives. How well are you doing at applying those same four marks of leadership? Using the scales below, with ten being high, evaluate yourself in each of those areas.

A leader has a clear recognition of needs.

| 1 | 2 | 3 | 4 | 5 | 6 | 7 | 8 | 9 | 10 |

A leader is personally concerned with the needs.

| 1 | 2 | 3 | 4 | 5 | 6 | 7 | 8 | 9 | 10 |

A leader goes first to God with the problem.

| 1 | 2 | 3 | 4 | 5 | 6 | 7 | 8 | 9 | 10 |

A leader is available to meet the need himself.

| 1 | 2 | 3 | 4 | 5 | 6 | 7 | 8 | 9 | 10 |

Which area do you think needs the most work right now? What can you do to cement that brick a little more securely in place? Be specific, and write it down as a goal.

2. We all know prayer is important—that isn't news to us. But even though prayer is a fundamental part of our lives, it's one that can generate a good deal of confusion.

For instance, have you ever wondered just how effective our prayers really are? Will God do whatever we request with no questions asked? Is there some magic formula that makes our prayers more effective? Are there certain elements, like worship or thanks, that we should try to include?

We may not fully understand the answers to these and other questions until we can ask God face to face. But there is much to be gained by probing into the scriptures and beginning to formulate your own view of prayer.

Starting with the prayer that was given to us as an example, why not make a personal study of this mysterious subject? You'll find that prayer in Luke 11:2–4. Write out both the elements and the attitudes that seem to be present in it. From there, a good concordance and perhaps a commentary will be helpful as you explore the other aspects of prayer the Bible informs us about.

Chapter 3

Preparation for a Tough Job

1.   We think of Nehemiah mainly as a leader, and he certainly was that—we see him in that role for the greater portion of his book. But before he was a leader, he was an employee. And it was the character he developed while still a servant that prepared him to be such a great leader.

With your pen in hand, study Nehemiah 2:1–10 for yourself. How would you describe Nehemiah's attitude toward his boss? How well do you think he'd do on a performance review? As you read, write down the characteristics that make Nehemiah an employee any manager would be glad to hire.

2.   Have you ever had a boss who was difficult to deal with? Maybe you're in that situation now. How do you handle it?

Part of the solution is following Nehemiah's example of being a good employee. We can find the other part in Proverbs 21:1. "The king's heart is like channels of water in the hands of the Lord. He turns it wherever He wishes."

The way to a man's heart may be through his stomach, but the way to a superior's heart is through the Lord. How much time have you spent grumbling about your boss as opposed to praying for him? Now would be a good time to start balancing out the scale!

Chapter 4

Getting off Dead Center

1.   Your public image is what you wear when you know people are watching. Your character is what you are when you think no one is looking.

It's a lot easier to polish up that public image than it is to concentrate on building true character. Yet Scripture tells us over and over again that God is more concerned with the state of our hearts than He is with the impression we make on other people.

But how are we to go about developing character? You've heard the old expression "you are what you eat." Along those same lines, Romans 12:2 suggests that we are what we *think*.

And do not be conformed to this world, but be transformed by the renewing of your mind, that you may prove what the will of God is, that which is good and acceptable and perfect.

And how are we to renew our minds? By thinking on things that are true, honorable, right, pure, lovely, of good repute, excellent, and worthy of praise (Phil. 4:8). To keep that "thought filter" in place, write Philippians 4:8 on an index card. Read it several times out loud until you know it by heart.

2. Are you having trouble motivating the people you lead? Your followers may be dragging their feet for one of two reasons. One, maybe they've never been told why their task is important. Two, maybe their job is too big and it overwhelms them.

Those Jews had been living with a broken-down wall for years before Nehemiah came along. How did he manage to get them excited about rebuilding it?

First, he gave them ownership of the problem—he helped them recognize the danger of their situation. Second, as we see in Nehemiah 3, he broke the job down into manageable tasks that were suited to the individuals. He assigned some to bring bricks, some to slap mortar, some to design gates.

What is the main task you'd like your followers to take ownership of? If you're a parent, it may be as basic as keeping the house clean. If you're in ministry, it may be getting workers to catch a vision for the lost. Whatever it is, what are some ways you can get them to see the need for themselves? How can you break the job down into tasks they can manage?

Don't forget to praise them for their achievements!

— 185 —

Chapter 5

Knocked Down, But Not Knocked Out

1. Are you thinking of investing your life in Christian ministry? Maybe you're already there. If so, you know that scattered among the feelings of joy and meaning and purpose are times of discouragement, frustration, and failure. But those things aren't necessarily signaling you that you've chosen the wrong path; they're probably just letting you know that things are normal! Paul, too, experienced those feelings.

    Over the next two weeks, read through 2 Corinthians, taking on one chapter a day. Keep a pen and notebook handy, and put your notes into two columns. *Attitudes Paul Had* and *Feelings Paul Had.* You're likely to gain new perspectives on the problems you'll face as you serve the Lord.

2. Sometimes it seems that the harder we try to do good, the more Satan tries to discourage us. Have you been feeling like you've been knocked down one too many times lately? Take another look at 2 Corinthians 4:8–10. Only this time, make it personal. In place of *we* and *our*, substitute *I* and *my*. In place of words like *persecuted* and *perplexed,* fill in your own current battles—for example, "I am swamped with impossible projects, but I will not stop trying!" Make this your own personal declaration of victory over the problems that threaten to knock you out.

3. Consistent criticism can eventually get under anybody's skin, and nothing would be more natural than to finally fly off the handle. But we've read enough of Proverbs—and had enough personal experience—to know that that response only serves to make things worse.

    Is there a critic in your life right now, a nagging, pestering complainer whose gripes and grumbles don't appear to be from God? Instead of biting your tongue, loosen it . . . in prayer. Bring the situation before God today and ask for His wisdom and patience in handling it.

Chapter 6

Discouragement: Its Cause and Cure

1. Halfway done is discouraging.

   Halfway through a long drive and you're tempted to find a hotel. Halfway into a relationship—past the first flutter of romance but not yet to the good part of commitment—and you're ready to break things off. Halfway through a difficult project, and you're trying to think of shortcuts.

   Getting halfway is easy; it's going all the way that's tough. But turn back to page 88 and read that Spurgeon quote again. Have you ever found that principle to be true in your own life? Have you ever stuck something out just a little longer than you thought you could and found the reward greater than you ever expected? Relive some of those memories before you go on.

   Are you at a halfway point right now? Maybe in your marriage, maybe in your career . . . is it really time to bail out? Don't make that decision on an impulse, and don't make it on an especially bad day. Make it on your knees. You may have to wait for the answer, as Nehemiah did in Persia, but start the process now, before you turn the page.

2. Look up Ecclesiastes 4:9–12. What does it have to say about the benefits of friendship?

   Are you a part of a "cord of three strands"? If you think of God as the second strand, who is your third? If the threads of friendship are frayed in your life, think of three things you can do this week to begin to repair or replace them.

3. When discouragement creeps up on your heart, one of the best things you can do is to recall the promises of the Lord. But it's hard to do that if you've never committed any to memory! Choose one or two to memorize today. If you have one in mind you've always meant to learn, you might pick that one. If you're not sure where to find one, the following references will give you a place to start.

Jeremiah 29:11	Psalm 25:10
Isaiah 26:3–4	Psalm 32:8
Philippians 4:6–7	Psalm 34:18

By the way, if you ever want to take on an overwhelming task—but an incredibly encouraging one—pick a book of the Bible, especially in the New Testament, and just try to make a list of all the promises God makes to us. You'll never doubt His love again!

Chapter 7

Love, Loans . . . and the Money Crunch

1. If I regard wickedness in my heart,
    The Lord will not hear. (Ps. 66:18)

The sins—the "wickedness" we regard in our hearts—are like the bricks in Nehemiah's wall. Only this wall is erected between us and God. Each time we sin, we lay down a brick . . . and each time we confess, we take the brick away. With every sin we choose to ignore, we raise a little higher the wall that shuts God out of our lives. His voice becomes a little harder to hear, His face a little harder to see. Eventually we forget His presence altogether, and we live as we please behind the privacy of our wall.

Are there a few bricks piled between you and God? A few secret sins you haven't gotten around to confessing? Now is the time to do it, before the wall is too high to see over.

2. Just as our sins build a wall between us and God, so our debts dig a hole we sometimes despair of climbing out of.

If you find yourself in that position, a helpful book is *Debt-Free Living* by Larry Burkett. If you want to avoid that situation and use your finances in a way that glorifies God, read *Master Your Money* by Ron Blue.

3.   The world around us is full of sin, and it doesn't bother to disguise it. As Christians, we have little trouble feeling indignant when non-Christian organizations blatantly oppose the principles we know God esteems. We sometimes even organize ourselves to fight back. But how do we respond to the sins of other Christians?

When a church friend brags about how he cheated on his income tax . . . when a Christian coworker passes on a filthy joke . . . when a believing relative calls you daily to gossip . . . how do you react? Do you overlook it? Merely cluck your tongue and feel glad you've overcome that problem? Decide it's none of your business?

Nehemiah didn't take his people's sins so lightly. In fact, he was outraged—and he let them know about it!

Based on Nehemiah's actions in this chapter, how do you think you should react next time a Christian invites you to participate in or applaud his sin? If you are in a group, role-play this scenario and possible ways to handle it.

Chapter 8

How to Handle a Promotion

1.   Nehemiah made the most of his high position; Solomon, for all his wisdom, failed miserably. Let's compare the two men to see how Nehemiah succeeded and where Solomon went wrong.

On another sheet of paper, make a chart with two columns, one headed "Solomon," the other headed "Nehemiah." Now read through the descriptions each man has recorded of his own time in office—you'll find Solomon's in Ecclesiastes 2:1–11 and Nehemiah's in Nehemiah 5:14–19. As you read, jot down details about how each man handled his promotion. At the bottom of your chart, write a description of how you think each man felt about himself when all was said and done.

2. Have you been pining away for a promotion yourself? There could, of course, be many reasons why God has seen fit to delay it. But just to eliminate one possible cause, evaluate your integrity in the job you currently have. On a scale of one to ten, ten being high, how would you rate yourself . . . closer to Solomon's selfish indulgence or closer to Nehemiah's impeccable standards?

1   2   3   4   5   6   7   8   9   10

Solomon   Nehemiah

If the standards you keep for yourself are pure and honest, you are to be truly congratulated—you are a rare employee indeed. But if you're like most of us, your office could use a little straightening up. Maybe fewer breaks here, more scrupulous records there . . . you know where your standards need dusting off.

What is one thing you could change this week to make your work more honoring to God?

3. Of the character qualities you've seen in Nehemiah so far, which do you think was the most helpful to him in maintaining his inner balance as he climbed up the ladder of success? Is this a quality you need more of as you prepare for possible future promotions? Choose a verse of Scripture that relates to this quality. Keep a copy of it in view on your desk to remind you to exercise that particular muscle of faith every day.

Chapter 9

Operation Intimidation

1. Have you ever stood in Nehemiah's shoes? You've been doing your darnedest to accomplish a worthwhile project, one you're convinced needs your attention, but you keep having to

fend off sneak attacks by people who want to undermine your work.

At times you just want to throw up your hands in defeat. Other times you keep standing firm, but with discouragement and frustration in your heart.

What you need at those times is a cheerleader. Someone to shout encouragement from the stands and give you pep talks when your enthusiasm wanes. How about listening to a voice from the past? As a measure of precaution for when those discouraging moments come or for a boost when you need it, copy the words of Winston Churchill onto a plaque or a card, or on whatever medium strikes your fancy: "Never give in, never, never, never, never."

2. Not only have we all been victimized by a vindictive tongue; we've exercised our own a time or two. Gossip is one of the most difficult habits to stay away from.

To help put controls on your tongue, look up the following verses from Proverbs and write out the principles they offer.

Proverbs 4:24
         6:16–19
         12:13, 17–19
         13:3
         15:1–2, 4, 23
         25:8–10, 15

Chapter 10

Revival at Water Gate?

1. Mary, Queen of Scots, once said of John Knox, "I fear his tongue and pen more than the armies of England."

What do the people in your life say about you? Read Matthew 5:13–16. In the literal sense, what are the qualities and purposes of salt? Of light? Write them down.

Now begin to think figuratively. If Christ calls you to be salt and light to the world around you, what is He asking you to do? How might those qualities of "salt" and "light" make a difference to the non-Christians you know? To the Christians? How do those differences relate to the idea of revival?

2.   Each of us has our own particular focal point when it comes to living the Christian life—you may have heard it referred to as a "life message." For some, it's evangelism. For others, it's obeying the Bible's guidelines for marriage. For you, it may be worship or steadfastness or the role of the Holy Spirit in our lives.

You're probably familiar with many of the hymns Charles Wesley gave the church; a partial list is on page 140 of this book. As you review the words of those songs, either in your memory or on the pages of a hymnal, what do you think Charles Wesley's life message was? How did it impact the world?

3.   You've likely spent years grooming the exterior of your life—providing for your family's needs, finding and furnishing an adequate home, educating or training yourself for a productive career. But after the spit and polish is applied, once your life is shiny and complete, do you, like the Jews, feel like something is still missing?

How do things look on the inside of your life? Has your heart been neglected in your striving for those other worthwhile things? Like the people of the newly remodeled Jerusalem, come with openness and repentance to hear the Word of God this week. Let revival start with you.

4.   In your dealings with other people, have you been trying to be everything to everybody? As a parent, maybe you've been trying to tutor your child in math when you've never mastered long division. As a Sunday school teacher, perhaps you're trying to organize a class missions project when administration simply isn't your gift.

It's noble of you to try to take everything on yourself. But it isn't necessary! That's what the Body of Christ is for. Even Nehemiah felt free to delegate the teaching of his people to Ezra.

What job are you trying to do that really isn't up your alley? Whose help could you request to take on that responsibility?

5.   The lives of great Christians down through the ages can be both intriguing and inspiring. Have you ever read about them? You might enjoy a devotional book that tells the stories of historical and contemporary Christians from around the world, some of whom will be familiar, others more obscure. It's called *Sacred Stories,* and it's written by Ruth A. Tucker.

Chapter 11

The Fine Art of Insight

1.   You may have heard the adage about people who sit in their pews Sunday after Sunday, listening to the sermon and even taking notes, but who leave every service with their lives virtually unchanged—it's been said that they just "sit, soak, and sour"!

That phrase describes people who have had a lot of input, but not much insight. How would you describe the difference between input and insight? Looking closely at your own life, which would you say you tend to get more of?

Whether you answered "input" or "insight," examine why you answered the way you did. You may find some of the reasons in the three specifics about gaining insight you read about on pages 151–152:

- It takes time.
- It takes the right people.
- It takes the right attitude.

2.   Perhaps you've had a hard time evaluating whether you're getting more input or insight. There is a way you can find out—look at the results! Rate yourself in the following two areas.

Am I walking in total obedience?

No way   Somewhat   Pretty much   As much as I know how

Have I discovered genuine happiness (contentment, joy, fulfillment)?

Not at all   Very Little   Some   A great deal

3.   Since none of us will truly "arrive" spiritually until we reach heaven, it's likely that one or more of the three areas above comes up a little short in your life. Which would you say is in most urgent need of change? What could you do about it?

If it's *time* you're lacking, maybe you need to reorganize your priorities. If it's *people,* maybe it would help to attend a conference or camp where you know the teaching will be exceptional—or perhaps you could simply begin attending a Bible study taught by someone who really knows the Scripture. If it's *attitude* you're struggling with, you're the one who can best say what you need to do—whether it means making up your mind to really listen to the sermons rather than doodling on your bulletin, or making an appointment to talk to your pastor or a counselor about some deep-down issues that are keeping you from being wholly open to God's Word.

You set the course. What is your plan of action?

Chapter 12

Putting First Things First

1.   Are you a thinker and a planner, or do you tend to shoot from the hip? There are times when spontaneity is a wonderful

quality, but important decisions and long-term plans require more careful consideration.

As you think about the people you're leading, whether they're your family or your employees, are there some issues you've been feeling a need to devote some deeper thought to? Have you been making some off-the-cuff decisions that are rapidly becoming policies simply because you haven't had time to think through a better solution? Maybe about your daughter's curfew or your son's behavior at school, perhaps about procedures at work.

List the major matters that have been falling through the cracks; then prioritize them, putting them in order of urgency. Which needs your attention first? When will you sit down and work that issue through?

2.   Have you been contemplating a major life change in the near future, such as a new job, a move, possibly marriage? Have you been thinking of tackling a big remodeling project or of taking on a new responsibility at church or in your community?

Risks like those are good for us; they're opportunities to exercise faith. But they're not meant to be entered into on an impulse.

Read Luke 14:28–31 and summarize what it says. Now, calculate the cost of your new endeavor—emotionally, financially, spiritually—and its feasibility. Is it practical? Is now the right time? Are you ready to pay the price?

3.   Did you catch that quote by Keith Miller on page 165? Go back and read it one more time, comparing it to 1 Corinthians 6:19–20. How do you think the two relate? In what way would we as Christians be different if we truly applied the passage from Scripture? How would you personally be different?

4.   We've studied briefly the covenant the Jews made before God in Nehemiah 10:28–39. Do you remember the major elements of that agreement? If not, review them by looking back through the chapter in our book.

Would you be willing to make a similar covenant with God?

Keeping in mind the *spirit* of the Jews' agreement rather than the actual details of it, see how the following New Testament verses parallel some of the ideas contained in that covenant. Then, if you're ready to make the commitment, write out your own covenant with God. This could be a good activity to do with your spouse or even your entire family, depending on the ages of your children.

Matthew 6:19–21
Acts 20:35
Ephesians 5:22–6:4
Colossians 3:18–21
Hebrews 13:15
1 Peter 1:14

Chapter 13

The Willing Unknowns

1. Think for a moment about the good things in your life—not the material things, but the emotional and spiritual things. The inheritance left you by the caring people who have crossed your path.

    Who are the "willing unknowns" in your life? Likely, there is no memorial to them in your home, but there surely is in your heart. Have you told those people lately what they've meant to you? If they are gone from this earth, have you thanked God recently for the riches He has given you through them?

    Take some time now to acknowledge these people whose love or guidance has made a difference in your life. Write a note, make a call, offer a prayer . . . but do it today.

2. Remember the very first exercise from the very first chapter of this book? If you had a hard time identifying yourself as a

leader, you may also struggle with the issue of unrecognized effort. Especially if you're leading in an unofficial capacity.

If you had no trouble identifying your followers . . . if your leadership position is up-front and highly visible, you may have to fight off the smugness that can so easily come with the approval of the people. In fact, you may even become addicted to it.

Which category can you most closely relate to?

Whichever it is, Matthew 6:21 has some words of wisdom for you. Paraphrase it, putting it in words that make it an ad monition that best fits your own situation.

3.   Was that last exercise a little discouraging? No matter how selfless we are, there's a little corner of our souls that has a built-in need for appreciation and recognition of a job well done. That's what keeps us going, ready to strive to do even better.

God doesn't ask us to deny that need. He just wants to be the one to fulfill it.

For an encouraging reminder of His constant recognition of our efforts, memorize Hebrews 6:10 or write it on a plaque or card. It will serve as a spiritual pat on the back at the very moment you really need one!

Chapter 14

Happiness Is on the Wall

1.   We have hearts that long for happiness, each and every one of us. Yet in our search for it, we so often turn the wrong way.

To what do you look for happiness? Be honest, now! Write down the first three things that come to mind.

God has, indeed, given us many good things to enjoy. But He means for our joy to be more lasting than the kind those transient pleasures can provide. Look up the verses below. As you read them, make a chart on another sheet of paper, listing the references on one side and the source of joy they describe on the other.

Romans 14:17
Galatians 5:22
James 1:2
1 John 1:4
Job 33:23–26
Psalm 21:6

2.   Happiness isn't just a hoped-for luxury in this world; it's a downright necessity! And, as we saw in our lesson today, it's contagious—and attainable.

How are you helping to spread the disease? Remember Philippians 4:8? If you keep your mind on the things that verse lists, you won't have much trouble spreading a smile.

Will you try to be infectious as you go through the rest of your day? Make it your goal to get a grin out of at least one other person!

Chapter 15

Taking Problems by the Throat

1.   When Nehemiah came back to Jerusalem and found Tobiah living in the house of God, he was livid. Why do you think that bothered him so much? What harm could it have done just to let Tobiah occupy a room or two in the temple? The following passages may help you with your answer.

Proverbs 13:20
1 Corinthians 15:33
2 Corinthians 6:14–18

According to what you've just read, is there anyone or anything that needs to be thrown out of your life?

2.   We Christians tend to shy away from anger. We also feel better keeping our noses out of other people's business—that is, if sticking our noses in might mean an unpleasant confrontation.

But Nehemiah didn't have those problems. He got good and angry when he saw his people breaking their promises to God—promises they'd made within his hearing. Where he saw wrong being done, he stepped in and did his best to stop it.

How are you when it comes to righteous indignation? Is there anything today that sets your blood boiling? Are you doing anything about it?

3.   Maybe you are dealing today with a problem that you need to take by the throat, but it's not the same kind of problem Nehemiah was faced with. Maybe, instead of your followers' misbehavior, it has to do with your own emotional or physical survival. Emotional injuries and physical disabilities can happen to anyone, even to leaders . . . like Beethoven.

Do you need a dose of the kind of determination that kept Beethoven at his keyboard? If so, take time out to give yourself a treat. Read Tim Hansel's *You Gotta Keep Dancin'*. Written by a man who lives daily with incredible physical pain, this book will be just the booster shot you need to get on your feet and give life one more heroic try.

Notes

1. John Bartlett, *Familiar Quotations* (Boston: Little, Brown and Company, 1955), p. 755.
2. Merrill F. Unger, *Unger's Bible Dictionary* (Chicago: Moody Press, 1959), p. 230.
3. A. W. Tozer, *The Root of the Righteous* (Harrisburg, Pa.: Christian Publications, Inc., 1955), p. 100.
4. Alan Redpath, *Victorious Christian Service* (New Jersey: Fleming H. Revell, 1958), p. 19.
5. Alfred B. Smith, "Got Any Rivers," *Making Melody* (St. Louis: Bible Memory Association Inc., 1954), p. 111.
6. Dorothy Price and Dean Walley, *Never Give In!* (Kansas City: Hallmark Cards Inc., 1967), pp. 3, 4, 6.
7. Bartlett, *Familiar Quotations*, p. 870.
8. *Ibid.*, p. 871.
9. J. Oswald Sanders, *Spiritual Leadership* (Chicago: Moody Press, 1967), p. 110.
10. J. B. Phillips, *Letters to Young Churches* (New York: The Macmillan Company, 1955), p. 76.
11. Theodore Roosevelt, Speech before the Hamilton Club, Chicago (April 10, 1899).
12. John Edmund Haggai, *How to Win Over Worry* (Grand Rapids: Zondervan, 1959), p. 144.
13. Charles Edison, "The Electric Thomas Edison," *Great Lives Great Deeds* (New York: Readers Digest Association, 1964), pp. 200-05.
14. Sanders, *Spiritual Leadership*, pp. 149-50.

15. C. S. Lewis, *The Four Loves* (New York: Harcourt, Brace & World, Inc., 1960), p. 169.
16. Clarence E. Macartney, *Preaching Without Notes* (New York: Abingdon Press, 1946), p. 178.
17. Bartlett, *Familiar Quotations*, p. 475.
18. C. Frederick Owen, *Abraham to the Middle-East Crisis*, (Grand Rapids: Eerdmans, 1957), pp. 56-7.
19. Sanders, *Spiritual Leadership*, p. 64.
20. Gerrit Verkuyl, ed., *The Modern Language Bible, The New Berkeley Version* (Grand Rapids: Zondervan, 1969), p. 208.
21. Peter F. Drucker, *Management* (New York: Harper & Row, 1974), pp. 301-02.
22. Ordway Tead, *The Art of Leadership* (New York: McGraw-Hill, 1935), p. 215.
23. Billy Graham, *World Aflame* (Garden City: Doubleday, 1965), pp. 22-3.
24. Keith Miller, *The Taste of New Wine* (Waco, Texas: Word Books, 1965), p. 79.
25. Billy Graham, *World Aflame* (New York: Doubleday, 1965), p. 31.
26. "... and I'll talk to you tomorrow." Booklet prepared by KNXT, Channel 2, in cooperation with the Los Angeles County Medical Association, December 1974, and distributed in conjunction with the Medix/KNXT, Channel 2, Los Angeles, television special "And I'll Talk to You Tomorrow."